'Not Pretty, I

Written and illustrated by Enid Bailey

To the happy memory of my parents
and to Derek, my constant support
and driving force

Published by

MELROSE
BOOKS

An Imprint of Melrose Press Limited
St Thomas Place, Ely
Cambridgeshire
CB7 4GG, UK
www.melrosebooks.com

FIRST EDITION

ISBN 978 1 907040 36 8

Printed and bound in Great Britain by:
CLE Digital Solutions. St Ives, Cambridgeshire

With special thanks to Stella Bolam.

my great-grandparents – Walter and Ellen Bell

Contents

1. Early Days at Deep Pits

Today, the busy roundabout at Ponds Forge in Sheffield ejects a continual rumble of cars and lorries up Duke Street and into City Road. Two-way traffic weaves between and around Supertram making this a hazardous route. Vast estates spread for miles on each side of the road.

City Road was not like this when Walter and Ellen Bell moved into the old farmhouse in 1896. The old farmhouse, almost surrounded by fields, jutted out into City Road. Any traffic, all horse-drawn, meandered around it. Not far from the farmhouse, in this little hamlet of Deep Pits, stood some old cottages. It was in one of these, on the 26th April 1911, that Emmie was born. Her parents, Thomas and Emily Evans, felt a deep sense of joy. Their first child, a son, christened Howard, had died soon after his first birthday. Howard would never be forgotten but now they had another child to cherish.

Emmie's grandparents at the farm were delighted too. Ellen had raised a big family and loved all her children. Two children had died at birth and she understood how much her daughter had grieved. She and Walter were happy to have this new grandchild so close.

Soon after 1900 new houses were built, here and there, on City Road. Don Terrace was built immediately opposite the farm. Thomas and Emily, with their baby girl, moved into the end house. A purpose-built dairy was attached to the side of the house. 'Deep Pits Dairy' was painted over the door. Thomas and Emily started a milk round. The horses for the milk float were stabled at the farm and Walter Bell's cows provided the milk. It was a good partnership.

From her birth, the farm was a second home to Emmie. As a baby in arms, she was carried round the farm to see the animals. She found the pigs particularly entertaining. There were pigs both on the farm and at Don Terrace. Thomas raised excellent pigs and soon began to win prizes. Emmie's first photograph was taken by a local reporter and published in the newspaper. Everybody laughed to see a contented baby sitting beside the fattest pig in South Yorkshire.

Emmie was never short of attention even though both of her parents were busy. At the farm, her two youngest uncles loved to make her laugh. They were still children when she was born. Arnold was thirteen and

Herbert was twelve. Arnold kept pigeons and, as soon as she was able, he encouraged her to hold one in her hands. She was unafraid and excited to feel the soft warmth of the birds. Herbert took her to feed the pigs and collect the eggs. They sang to her. Arnold played the violin and taught her to sing 'There is sunshine in my soul today'. Their duet earned a round of applause from the family.

A highlight in the farming year was the Norton Agricultural Show. Walter Bell was very proud of his matching shire horses, Brightside and Carbrook, the name of the local Co-op. While Emmie was still very young, he entered them in the show. Arnold and Herbert looked forward to this event and pestered their father to let them braid the horses' manes on the great day. Walter had always attended to this crowning glory of his precious horses himself but agreed, with the condition that they practised until they were perfect.

"It's not as easy as it looks," he said. "Plaiting the mane with straw is an old art and it cannot be learned overnight."

The problem that Arnold and Herbert faced was that the hardworking horses were not often available for practice. They were discussing this difficulty while they watched Emmie feeding the ducks. Then Arnold, gazing at Emmie, had a sudden, brilliant idea. Emmie's long, chestnut curls, the pride of her mother's life, would be ideal for plaiting! Emmie, happy to oblige her adored uncles, sat on the table in the washhouse and allowed them to part her hair down the middle. They each tackled a plait. Dividing her hair into three strands was not too difficult but weaving the twisted straw in and out was another matter. Emmie's hair was fine and slipped out of the plait. The straw split and became entangled. Arnold gathered more straw and tried again. This time he produced a plait but it resembled a hedgehog.

"I think you do it like this," he said.

"No – you need more straw," insisted Herbert and tried a plait at the other side. Emmie began to protest.

"It pulls! It pulls!" she squeaked.

"Dad's right," said Herbert. "It's not as easy as it looks."

Emmie began to cry and the boys to panic. They tried to remove the straw but Emmie only cried harder and their efforts made matters worse. Footsteps warned them that Emily was coming and they knew they were in trouble. She was horrified and gave her brothers the sharp side of her tongue. She realised that no amount of combing would remove the straw and whisked Emmie off to Kings in Sheffield. There, the hair and the straw were cut away and Emmie came home looking completely different, her hair cut close to her head.

"Whose little girl are you?" asked Thomas and gave her a cuddle. "It will soon grow again," he consoled Emily. For a long time after that, Emmie was known as Little Bob.

Emily soon forgave her brothers and on the day of the show she allowed Emmie to watch with Grandma Bell as Grandad brought the two big shire horses into the stack yard to groom them. Arnold and Herbert washed them down and brushed their coats.

"You can help too," said Arnold. "Up you go!" Emmie was perched high on Brightside's back.

"Hold tight to his mane," warned Herbert and he pushed a pair of Grandma Bell's old silk bloomers into her hand. Silk was well-known for producing a good shine. "Rub hard!" they urged. Emmie clenched her teeth in her determination to make Brightside beautiful. She clung on tightly with one hand and the horse, seeming to know he held a special burden, stood patiently still. Emily, coming into the yard, swallowed hard when she saw Emmie in her lofty position. But she realised that Emmie was enjoying her activity and didn't interfere. Grandma Bell's old silk bloomers were very grimy when Emmie had finished and Emmie's own bloomers were ready for washday too. She tumbled down into Arnold's arms, her face flushed with excitement. From that moment, she was passionate about horses.

Emmie was instructed to stand back with Grandma and she was not allowed to help when Arnold and Herbert washed the horses' heavy, feathery feet in buckets of water. She laughed when Carbrook suddenly set off around the yard with his foot still in the clanking bucket. She watched as their feathers were combed and fluffed out and as the boys oiled the horses' hooves to make them shine. But it was Walter who braided their manes with straw!

Finally, Walter, Arnold and Herbert went into the house to wash and change. They emerged looking well-scrubbed, smart and tidy. Brightside and Carbrook were harnessed to an unusually clean cart, their horse brasses gleaming. Walter took the reins and his sons sat one on each side of him. They all looked truly splendid. Emmie was very proud of them.

2. Pig in a Sock

A sketch was made of Emmie in 1914 and the artist caught a certain gleam of mischief in her eyes. Standing still with her bucket and spade must have been a lot to ask. Her mother considered that she was naughty but her misdemeanours could not have been very serious. Emmie was brought up an only child but she was not spoilt. Now and then there were childish tantrums but a wet dishcloth smacked round her legs soon settled those. Thomas and Emily were strict parents.

Emmie did not have many toys and preferred playing with Jack, the Old English sheepdog. He was her constant guard and companion, ready to join in all her games. The family cat was not so cooperative and did her best to give Emmie a wide berth. Naturally Emmie seized every opportunity to capture the cat. The angry creature objected to tight fingers grasping her tail or being hoisted suddenly around the middle while she was dozing. Emmie was warned so frequently, "She'll scratch you!" that she told customers in the dairy, "We have a dog – Jack – and a scratchyer!"

One day in the dairy Emily heard the cat wailing and spitting. She rushed into the kitchen to find Emmie forcing the cat into the old dolls' pram.

"She'll scratch you!" Emily called automatically but the warning was too late. The cat's claws dug into Emmie's arms and Emmie screamed, dropping the cat, which escaped through the back door. There was no sympathy of course and Emmie's bottom lip wobbled. Just at that moment, Thomas put his head round the door and said, "Do you want to see the piglets, Emmie?" The scratch was forgotten as Thomas took her hand. They crossed the communal yard and the track behind the outside lavatories, passed Thomas's workshop and made their way up the long sloping garden. All the houses in Don Terrace had long gardens. Thomas and Emily's garden was wider than the rest to accommodate the dairy. Each house had a concrete slab at the top of the garden designed for pigsties. Their owners built their own sties with sleeping parts and an outside pen with proper drainage. There was an alcove at the front with a chute where the swill was poured into a trough. Thomas kept pigs in his own sty and rented some of his neighbours' sties. He lifted Emmie up to see the big sow laid in a bed of clean straw. A line of small piglets suckled urgently. Emmie was intrigued by their smallness, their pinkness, and the way they all moved their tiny trotters. Her eyes picked out an extra small one struggling to find a teat.

"Look," she said. "Poor little pig!"

Thomas was already looking at the tiny piglet. There seemed to be a runt in every litter. It would not survive in the sty and he very much doubted that it would live anyway. Usually he gave such piglets a chance, feeding them drops of milk in the house. He leaned over, lifted it out and gave it to Emmie to hold. Emmie felt for the first time the sheer silkiness of a piglet's skin. She carried it into the house with the greatest of care. She watched as her mother tried to squeeze a few drops of milk into its mouth. She listened attentively as her mother told her, "This little pig is not very well. He needs to be wrapped up warmly and lie down quietly." Emily put the piglet into one of Thomas's old socks and laid him – to Emmie's delight – in her dolls' pram. "The cat can have some respite now," thought Emily.

Emmie covered the piglet tenderly and wheeled the pram around gently, peeping regularly at her charge. Everyone was glad she was so occupied. The peace could not last. A few days later, Aunt Florrie came over from the farm and looked in the pram.

"Sithee!" she exclaimed. "How long has that child been wheeling a dead pig around?"

Of course Emmie could not believe the piglet was dead and was distraught at its removal. To learn that piglets die was a hard lesson but it was one she soon accepted. After all, at the top of the garden, fifteen noisy little piglets, very much alive, demanded her attention.

3. The Lord Mayor of Deep Pits

From her birth, Grandad Bell was a central figure in Emmie's life. Once she found her feet she followed him into the cowsheds and watched him at work in the barn. She sat between him and Grandma Bell by the fireside and climbed on his knee to smell the flower he often wore in his coat.

Farmer Bell was well-known locally. He had a big heart and a big personality. He was a busy farmer and a family man. Walter loved children and allowed his fields to be used for their Sunday school treats and gala days. On Whit Monday, when the children ran races and sports, he provided sweets for them all. Emmie was the apple of his eye and sometimes he took her with him on his errands. Lifted up high and tucked in firmly beside Grandad on the driving seat, she waited as he took up the reins. The slight lurch as they set off always made her laugh. It was exciting watching the horse's head tossing and hearing the clippety-clop of the hooves. Sometimes, coming home, she slept, still feeling the rhythm of the horse trotting and the trap swaying.

On one of these excursions Emmie's mother did not realise Grandad had taken her, causing Emily great alarm. She remonstrated with him. Not only had he taken Emmie without a 'by-your-leave', she was only wearing her petticoat!

"He's a law unto himself!" she grumbled to Thomas.

Farming was a hard life but Walter Bell considered himself very fortunate. Life had not always treated him so well. The story of his early years was strange and sad. His mother, Louisa, came from Retford where she lived with her parents, George Bell and his wife, Elizabeth, who had been born in Nottinghamshire. When she was seventeen, Louisa, so the story goes, was seduced by a wealthy, itinerant cattle dealer. Subsequently she gave birth to Walter in 1857. Eventually she married a man called Goodman and Walter went with them to live at Sprotborough. More children were born – Polly, Ada, Joe, and another Walter.

Then a further upheaval occurred in Walter's life. He told this story to his grandchildren.

"I was sold to a farmer in Gilding Wells when I was seven years old. My mother was heartbroken. I was not treated as one of the family. I only had one pair of socks and I could not wear them in the house. I had to peg them on the line."

Walter was adamant that he was sold. Maybe there were too many mouths to feed. In spite of being 'farmed out', Walter did not lose touch with his family. He rarely talked about his growing-up years, but he must have worked his way up because when he married Ellen, the marriage certificate stated that he was a carter. To become a tenant farmer was a big step forward. For a time they lived at Cricket Inn Road and later moved to Ecclesfield. Ellen's mother, Mary Ann Crowder, had thirteen children. She wondered if Ellen, too, would have a 'baker's dozen'.

"I'll have my own dozen, thank you," said Ellen and she did. As well as the two children who died at birth, she bore William, Walter, Eliza Ellen, Emily (Emmie's mother), Florice, Ethel Victoria, Ada Louise, Edith May, Arnold, and Herbert.

It is likely that Walter Bell inherited his natural father's skill with cattle. He had a reputation in Deep Pits and the surrounding areas for his expertise. He loved his cows. An artist came to paint his favourite cow. The artist at work was a great attraction in the stack yard. Emmie watched too and saw the picture proudly hung on the wall.

Walter was well-known at cattle markets and auctions. One day, at an auction, he was sitting next to a well-dressed man who asked his advice on buying cattle. Walter was pleased to help and discovered that his new friend was the Duke of Norfolk. Walter was one of the Duke's many tenant farmers but they had never met. After the auction, the Duke took Walter for a meal. On another occasion, Walter returned the compliment, taking the Duke to an establishment frequented by local farmers. At home, Ellen wanted to hear all the details.

All the men had sat at a long table. Walter was at the head of the table and the Duke was seated on his right. A large joint was brought for Walter to carve. He gave the Duke a good helping. The Duke was so impressed by Walter's carving that he invited him to carve the meat at some of his functions and to serve the wine.

So, from time to time, Walter performed these duties for the Duke of Norfolk and on one of these occasions the Duke gave Walter a silver corkscrew bottle opener.

Walter and Ellen were proud that they managed to pay for their children to attend school. The cost was fourpence a week for each child. They wanted them to have the education they never had. Neither of them could read.

When he was not working, Walter usually had a flower in his coat and enjoyed a cigar. It amused him, and the neighbours, to tell people he was the Lord Mayor of Deep Pits! Some people believed him. The little boy who was sold at the age of seven had come a long way.

4. Shadows and Sunshine

Emmie was still very small when tragedy struck the Bell family. Her mother's sister, Eliza Ellen, died suddenly in Newcastle-upon-Tyne. Eliza Ellen, sometimes called Bella, but always known to her sisters and brothers as Nellie, was the oldest of Walter and Ellen's daughters. Emily had always been protective of her gentle older sister. They had been very close in age and companionship and Emily felt her loss deeply. Walter and Ellen were devastated to lose their first daughter but, even in their grief, their main concern was for the two little girls who were left motherless in Newcastle. Phyllis was five and Nellie was four. Their father, Thomas Mansfield, dared not give up his job to care for them and there was no one able to watch over them while he was at work. Walter and Ellen, without hesitation, offered them a home. Ellen, no longer young, profoundly deaf and unused to travelling, faced up to the daunting train journey north to fetch the children.

Naturally, they cried when they left their distressed father and they were afraid of the train. Above all, they wanted their mother. How was Ellen to comfort them? She was a stranger to them even if she was their grandmother and to be up-rooted from all that was loved and familiar was a traumatic experience. Since their mother's funeral was to take place in Sheffield, her coffin was travelling with them. It was laid on the seat in the railway carriage facing Grandma Bell who sat with a sad little girl on each side. Staring at the coffin, the journey seemed interminable. It was cold, there was no corridor and the carriage was unlit on that dark winter's night. Eventually the children slept for a while until the train lurched them back into reality and there were more tears. The bleak journey dragged on and the presence of the coffin seemed unbearable.

At last, after an eternity, they arrived in Sheffield to be met by Grandad Bell and his two sons, William and Walter. The three men hoisted the coffin on to the coal cart and William and Walter drove away sadly with their sister's body. Grandad Bell had brought the pony and trap. His strong arms lifted each little granddaughter into the trap. Grandma climbed in and wrapped a blanket round their knees. The dreadful train journey was over.

At the farmhouse, Emily and Thomas had made sure a good fire was burning to welcome them. Grandma Bell brought the shy little girls near to the blazing fire to warm themselves and Phyllis tripped and burned her hand on the hearth. Not a good start!

The big kitchen was full of people all wanting to cheer these little girls while their own hearts were full of sadness. This difficult situation was overcome by Emmie who, with no understanding of the situation, was her normal self – a rumbustious toddler playing with the dogs. Phyllis and Nellie were distracted by her antics and joined her in fussing Jack and Rags, the farmhouse terriers. The dogs were an immediate comfort and the three little girls' immediate friends.

As the days passed, Phyllis and Nellie settled in, surrounded by love and affection. They grew to know their many aunts, uncles and cousins. Emmie remained their favourite playmate. Together they found all kinds of amusements. Grandma Bell, after bringing up so many children, was not house-proud. It did her good to hear them laughing as they slid across her long polished dining table on their tummies. The six stone steps leading from the farmhouse kitchen up to the front room were fine for 'let's pretend' games. Nellie and Phyllis, with Emmie between them, practised counting as they jumped up and down the steps. On sunny days, they fed the ducks on the farm pond and climbed the willow tree. Arnold and Herbert gave them piggybacks. The farm became their home and Newcastle a fading memory. Having two little girls made a lot of work for Grandma Bell, but their faces reminded her of the daughter she had lost and caring for them brought her great solace. Emily frequently took them across to Don Terrace where they had meals with Emmie. Sometimes, for a treat, there was Emily's delicious homemade ice cream. On Sundays, the whole family went to church.

Phyllis and Nellie were part of the family when, two years later, a message arrived. Their father was marrying again and he would be coming to fetch the girls. Grandma Bell hoped that his new wife would love them. She found it hard to part with them. Emmie missed them terribly but there were other friends and playmates. She was not short of company but she never forgot Nellie and Phyllis.

*　　*　　*　　*　　*

In the days that followed the departure of the girls, Thomas and Emily made an extra effort to keep Emmie occupied. They were pleased to find she knew most of her letter sounds and could write some of them. She could recognise and write her own name. Emmie loved books but she only possessed a few. Children's books were an expensive luxury. Imagine her delight when a good customer passed on a box full of picture books! Happy hours were spent telling herself stories even though she couldn't read the words.

Soon after receiving this wonderful gift, Emmie developed a high temperature and rapidly became very ill. She was taken to Lodge Moor Isolation Hospital in Sheffield. Thomas and Emily, having already lost a son, were filled with dread.

On arrival at hospital, Emmie's head was shaved as a matter of routine. A few curls were left around her face. She was in hospital for many weeks. From time to time Emmie, lying weakly in bed, thought she saw her mother's face peering through the window. Snowflakes were falling round her head. Confused by her illness, Emmie was unsure that her mother was real. Gradually emerging from this dangerous stage, she knew her parents came to see her. Parents were allowed to wave to their children through the window but could not visit the wards. Lying in a cot, with nothing to interest her, Emmie watched for her mother. One day her mother seemed to be telling her to read a book. Her lips were mouthing "Read a book" and her hands were pretending to turn pages. Emmie smiled at this pantomime. Eventually a book appeared. Was it from her mother? Emmie did not know but it became the centre of her life.

Each page showed a picture of a farm animal with the name beneath. Staring at the letters Emmie began to understand how to build the words. The next step was to create stories in her imagination, telling herself, "The pig said to the cow…", "The cow said to the donkey…" and so on.

At last Emmie was moved out of isolation and put with other children who were also on the road to recovery. Special stockings were given to her to encourage the peeling of the skin. They were very itchy and had to be removed several times a day. She had to learn how to turn them inside out and shake out the dead skin. On the great day that she was allowed to go home, she was given two baths, each containing strong disinfectant.

The whole family was glad to have her back.

"Our little ray of sunshine is home again," said Thomas to Emily. Everyone was thankful to have her home again but shaken to find the effects of institutionalisation. Her conversation was gibberish and consisted of "The cow said to the pig". Her stomach was enlarged and she ate slice after slice of bread! It was some time before she was herself again. Emmie then realised that her precious box of books was missing. Thomas and Emily had been dreading this moment. The box and its precious contents had been burned to prevent the spread of infection. Of course, Emmie cried and her parents tried to lift her spirits. They told her, "You will soon be going to school and there are hundreds of books at school. You will be able to read them all."

With that, Emmie had to be satisfied.

5. Farewell, Boys!

While there were trials and tribulations at Deep Pits, terrible sufferings were taking place in the world at large. The First World War began in 1914. Like many other young men, Arnold Bell made the decision to serve his country. On the day that he left, his oldest brother, William, came to bid him farewell. He brought his son, Jack, who was the same age as Emmie. The two small children stood side-by-side watching him lace up his boots and, although they didn't understand what was happening, they sensed the seriousness of the situation and the unhappiness of their family. Walter, Ellen and the family took turns to hug him. He smiled cheerfully but few words were spoken. They gathered outside the farm gates to see him march away. Emmie and Jack watched him until he was out of sight, a picture that was imprinted on their minds. His brother and inseparable companion, Herbert, went part of the way with him. The family turned away quietly. Walter's arm was round Ellen's shoulder. They were both wondering silently if they would ever see him again.

Emmie's mother, knowing how fond Arnold was of his little niece, took her to have her photograph taken. Emily wrote on the back 'To Uncle Arnie from Little Bob'. They posted the picture to him. Arnold was in the York and Lancaster Regiment.

The following year, a repeat farewell took place, but this time it was Herbert who left to join the South Staffordshire Regiment.

The family thought of the boys constantly but life at home had to go on. Emmie started school.

The Manor Board School was built in 1876 and is situated just below Manor Castle. It is not far from the cemetery with its long walls and impressive entrance designed for sober queues of horses and carriages. It was a long walk for Emmie on her first day at school in 1916. Clutching Nellie Jeffcock's hand, her feelings were a mixture of fear and trepidation. Nellie was two years older than Emmie and lived 'up the yard'. Nellie showed her into her classroom and disappeared quickly. Emmie was left gazing around at the high, exposed beams and the large fireplace. An enormous fireguard stood there. On wet winter days, dripping clothes hung over it to dry.

After a long morning, Nellie collected Emmie and took her home for lunch. Then there was another long walk back to school. School meals were not provided but some children were allowed to bring their own pies. The caretaker stuck name labels in them. They were heated for dinner.

Emmie did not make an auspicious start to her studies. How was she to know that the handful of beans on her desk was to count and not to eat? At home, she complained tearfully to her parents,

"They tasted horrid and they were hard to swallow and the teacher was cross!"

Gradually she settled in and became independent. She needed to be so because her parents had to leave early to deliver the milk. Grandparents and good neighbours were close by but she was expected to attend to herself. Her breakfast was left ready, but she had to wash, dress and brush her hair alone. She had to be ready for school on time.

Dressing was a complex affair. First came a woollen, short-sleeved vest that buttoned to the neck and then combinations. Emmie hated combinations! It was a struggle to climb into this all-in-one garment with

15

elbow-length sleeves. The buttons were fiddly and the flap at the back irritated her. Next came the Liberty bodice, essential after rheumatic fever – more buttons! The black stockings she attached to them were the best that Ashworth's could sell. Over these she pulled fleecy-lined knickers with elasticated waist and legs. They were much patched. Once her petticoat was over her head, she pulled on a skirt and jumper.

Emmie had been told firmly by her mother that she was 'not pretty, but pleasant'. She had no illusions about her appearance and no vanity but she knew her hair was much admired. When it was brushed, she lifted a thick strand of hair and threaded a ribbon under it. To tie the ribbon, she pressed her head against the cupboard door. This habit formed a shiny patch on the door! Sometimes when she was battling with the ribbon, her best friend Joe arrived to tie it for her. Joe Smith lived in the yard too and called for her every morning. Going to school became a routine and life continued as usual at Deep Pits. Farmer Bell carried on planting potatoes, harvesting corn, and bringing home the cows. Thomas and Emily delivered the milk.

Grandma Bell, in the farmhouse, found life too quiet. Her unmarried daughter, Florice, still lived at home but with Phyllis and Nellie back in Newcastle and Arnold and Herbert far away, the house was not the same. She missed the teasing of her youngest sons and the continual questions of the girls. Thank goodness she still had Emmie!

One Saturday, Emmie was sitting on the farmhouse doorstep when a boy on a bike pedalled through the gate.

"Mrs Bell live here?" he asked abruptly.

"Yes," said Emmie, rather startled. She called her Grandma, and the boy handed her an envelope. Grandma Bell closed her eyes and turned blindly back into the kitchen. She sank suddenly into the armchair. Emmie was only six and didn't understand but she knew by Grandma's white face that something was wrong. One of Arnold's pigeons flew into the kitchen and Emmie tried to distract Grandma.

"Perhaps he's come to tell us Arnold is coming home."

"No, Emmie," said Grandma gently. "He's come to tell us Arnold is not coming home." Then she looked at Emmie. "Go and find Grandad. Tell him I want him."

Arnold had been killed in action on the 15th June 1917. He was nineteen. He was buried in the Albuera Cemetery, Bailleuil-sire-Berthoult near Arras in France. His few belongings were eventually sent home. The treasured photo of Emmie was amongst them.

The following year, on 14th August 1918, Herbert died in Germany, a prisoner of war. The whole family, like so many other families, was devastated. Their terrible sense of loss was to be passed down from generation to generation.

6. 'A Real Honour'

Before Deep Pits had its own church, the village people attended churches in other areas. When John Oxley, John Ironside and other local benefactors succeeded in building the new Methodist Church and Institute at Deep Pits, everyone rejoiced, brought together not only for worship, but also for social activities. The two plain wooden buildings, which formed the shape of a 'T', were joined by a covered walkway. The church was erected opposite the top end of City Road Cemetery, close to Spring Lane. The opening day was a momentous occasion and the ladies who served the tea had their photographs taken. Emmie's mother, like all the other ladies, wore a white apron. The front building was a simple hall with a stage. A lectern and benches for the congregation provided for Sunday Services. The vestry behind the stage doubled as dressing rooms for concerts. The long, undivided room – the Institute at the back – was in use every night. To the left was the section for whist drives and social gatherings. On the right a more austere atmosphere prevailed. Two massive snooker tables, with shaded lights, stood between raised viewing platforms. Snooker cues, engraved with their owners' names, hung on the wall. There was a permanent air of concentration. When the grown-ups were playing whist or snooker, Emmie and her friends went on tiptoe if they had reason to go into the Institute. Occasionally they stood quietly to watch for a little while, knowing that the snooker players were too absorbed to notice them. They found it particularly fascinating to watch Mr Dickson, a much-respected man. He had served with the Royal Norfolk Regiment and lost his left arm in 1916. He never spoke of his injury but astonished everyone by his dexterity. He tackled snooker with his customary determination and made a wooden block with a groove in the top on which to rest his cue. He was an expert player, and although Emmie didn't understand the game she could see how skilful he was. Everyone said that he could do more with one arm than most people could do with two. The pulpit-shaped lectern in the church had been made by Mr Dickson. No one would have guessed it had once been a wardrobe!

Both church and social activities flourished. The war was over and people were determined to make the most of their lives. Sport was popular. Deep Pits Institute Cricket Team boasted some good players. Ron Wolfendon was a left-handed bowler, reputed to be able to spin a ball to ninety degrees! His father was the umpire. Others, not so efficient, were given opportunities to play. Fatty Greg – unkindly but appropriately named – could only bowl vertically!

The Institute had its own tennis courts and a football team too. Emmie's father was not a sportsman but he was a supporter and chief handyman at the Institute. Emmie was not fascinated by sport but she loved the many theatrical ventures. There was great excitement when a fancy dress party was proposed.

"What can I be?" she asked her mother.

"What about 'Bedtime'?" suggested Emily.

Costumes were very homespun and Emmie was content to wear her nightie and slippers. Her mother looked quite dashing in a policeman's borrowed helmet. Thomas went along in his everyday wear.

The party was a packed and hilarious affair. Towards the end of the evening, a photograph was taken. Assembling those present into some kind of order was a lengthy procedure, but at last everyone was crammed into position. The children were mostly shepherded to the front and their elders were seated or stood, squeezed together on the stage. One lady, particularly squashed, called out in panic, "I'm not on my feet!"

A gruff voice responded, "No, you're on mine!"

The more agile ones climbed precariously onto tables and even higher perches. Emmie sat comfortably on the front row. A large placard, reading 'For everything up-to-date apply Deep Pits Institute' was held up proudly. When all was ready the mirth and merriment suddenly ceased. Photography was taken seriously. Cameras were not commonplace and they were regarded with some awe. Only Thomas smiles out of the resulting picture.

The Church and Institute provided activities for all ages and stages. Everyone was considered to have some talents to contribute. Concerts abounded. They were given annually by the choir, the ladies of the 'Bright Hour', and the 'Sewing Circle'. The gentlemen produced one: 'The Men's Effort'.

One of the first productions at Deep Pits was 'The Magic Key'. Emmie was very proud of her mother who was on stage in a gypsy costume. Emmie and her cousin, Norah, clapped very loudly. There were special productions for the Sunday school and Emmie was always delighted to take part.

Soon after the war, the 'Girls' Life Brigade' and the 'Boys' Life Brigade' companies were formed. Emmie joined immediately and the Brigade became an important part of her life. She made her promise seriously 'to seek, serve and follow Christ'. In the early days of the Brigade at Deep Pits, people were very aware of the need for first aid and nursing due to the appalling injuries soldiers had received in the war. Many men had returned blinded or maimed. One of the purposes of the Life Brigades was, as the name implies, to save lives. First Aid training was an important part of the discipline. That training was to stand Emmie in good stead.

Everywhere, people were beginning to pick up the threads of life again and the community of Deep Pits found a renewed enthusiasm for many activities, but they did not forget those who had died. Ten young men from Deep Pits, including Emmie's two uncles, had never returned. There was a general desire to create a memorial to them. People were eager to give to this cause, but most families were struggling to make ends meet. Thomas kept a collection box on the milk float and on Saturday mornings Emmie helped him to collect pennies and halfpennies. It took a long time to save a sufficient amount to purchase a simple, scroll-shaped

stone engraved with the names of the men who had given their lives. One evening Emmie came home from Brigade with special news for her parents.

"I have been chosen to lay a wreath on the stone," she told them.

A mixture of pride and concern flew across their faces.

"Why have they chosen you?" asked Thomas.

"Because I am the only one at G.L.B. to have two relatives on the stone," said Emmie. Thomas and Emily relaxed. That was a good reason for her selection.

"It's a real honour," they said.

The stone was placed by the side of the church porch in a small square of garden and crowds of people stood in City Road for its commemoration on Remembrance Sunday. Emily had made sure that Emmie was looking smart.

"Take your time," she advised her daughter, as she gave Emmie's hair a special brushing. "It would not be reverent to rush it."

It was a very solemn occasion and a brave contingent of soldiers in uniform stood to attention. Others, who had survived the war, stood quietly, as dark memories returned. The girls, in their neatly pressed uniforms, lined up behind their flag. A band played, their instruments gleaming in the sunshine. Prayers were said. Local dignitaries laid their wreaths and then it was Emmie's turn.

She stepped forward, a small figure at the top of the church steps. The sun shone on her chestnut hair, and on the bright poppies in her hand. She gazed at the stone and her eyes lingered on the names Arnold Bell and Herbert Bell. For a moment the crowds, the band, and the soldiers were all forgotten. All she saw were the laughing faces of Arnold and Herbert. Then, with the greatest of care, she balanced her poppies beneath the stone. Stepping back, she gave her smartest salute. There was silence and then a bugle played 'The Last Post'.

7. The Organ Grinder

"Emmie! The Tingalari Man is coming!"

Jessie Jeffcock stood in the doorway quivering with excitement. Emmie ran to join her just as the organ grinder emerged from the passage into the shared back yard. He was accompanied by a small band of children who had tagged on to him as he crossed over from Deep Pits yard. Joe and Nellie were already bouncing up and down in front of him. Lily and Rene Hanson came running down their back garden with Mary Battams who was

pulling her little sister along. Parents and neighbours were gathering on their freshly donkey-stoned doorsteps.

The monkey was the big draw. His bright round eyes watched the children as keenly as they watched him. Dressed in red cap, waistcoat and trousers, he chattered into the organ grinder's ear. Then the music began! The man turned the handle of his barrel organ and began to sing along to the tunes, his black, curly moustache waving as he sang. His eyes flashed and he stopped frequently to joke with the children. They skipped and danced to the music and their elders clapped. All cares were forgotten. After a while the organ grinder paused. The monkey held out his tin mug for pennies. There were titbits for the monkey too, and he scampered about collecting them. Then, suddenly, he leapt on to the organ, scattering the onlookers, and the music began again. Emmie went closer to look at the organ and felt her hair ribbon slyly undone. She laughed and so did all the other children.

"He's a rascal!" said the organ grinder. Then he turned to go. "See you next year!"

Emmie's mother passed her a sandwich to give to the organ grinder and he gave her a smile and went on his way. The children watched him wistfully as he disappeared up the hill, a colourful character. No one then dreamed of radio or television and such an interlude was entertainment indeed.

Many years later, Emmie would recall this exotic visitor as she read to her children from a poem by Robert Louis Stevenson:

> The children sing in far Japan
> The children sing in Spain
> The organ with the organ man
> Is singing in the rain.

*   *   *   *   *

The back yard at Don Terrace was a favourite gathering place for the children. Sometimes they sat in a row, dangling their legs, on the brick wall by Emmie's kitchen window. Emily warned them, "Don't fall into the horse trough."

A large, stone horse trough stood on the other side of the wall beneath the dairy window. Four houses shared the back yard and the central passage. On rainy days the children played in the passage. A game of their own making was 'good eggs and bad eggs'. Their shouting echoed in the passage and this was not a popular game with the grown-ups.

Across the yard, each family had a lavatory and a coalhouse. A track ran across behind the lavatories, providing a place to play races. The long gardens beyond extended their playing area. There were hiding places in abundance and the cry "Coming, ready or not!" could be heard almost every day.

When the children tired of games they visited the pigs. One such day, as they hung over the sty walls talking to the pigs, Joe said, "Let's fetch some coal to give the pigs a treat." At the mention of the word 'coal', there was a chorus of grunting from their piggy friends.

Lily Hanson said, "We'll get into trouble!" but feeding the pigs coal was such a temptation that her warning was ignored. Soon all the children were sidling, hopefully unnoticeably, into their own coal sheds to fill their pockets with coal. Back at the sty, there was some debate about which pig should be fed by which child.

"Emmie should choose first," decided Joe. "These are her pigs."

"I like them all," said Emmie.

"I like that big one," said Jessie. "Can I have him?"

At last the matter was settled and the pigs' treat began. Piece by piece, the coal was dropped over the wall and the pigs snuffled around greedily.

"They think it's seaside rock!" Lily giggled as the coal was crunched loudly and with grunts of great appreciation. Emmie's pig, wanting more, stood up straight with his front trotters on the wall. His long snout turned from side to side and the children looked up at him.

"He's saying thank you!" laughed Amy.

Suddenly Emmie glanced down the garden. Her father was starting up the path with a bucket of swill.

"Dad's coming!" she exclaimed, and as one the children disappeared behind the sty, but Thomas was not to be deceived. He saw a stray lump of coal and the hem of a red coat.

"Come out!" he demanded and looked at them severely. They hung their heads. "Up to your tricks again! How many times do we have to tell you that coal is expensive? Now leave the pigs alone!"

Suitably admonished, the children retreated. Emmie knew she would face another scolding. Strangely, only the expense of the coal mattered. No one was ever concerned about this peculiar addition to the pigs' diet.

*   *   *   *   *

Emmie and her friends may have had plenty of freedom during the week but Sundays were a different matter. At home, the Sabbath day was regarded as a day of rest; not too strictly, but quiet play was expected. Emmie had two Victorian scrapbooks, which she was allowed to look at on Sundays. They were full of flying cherubs, little girls in muffs skating, boys with sailor collars riding hobbyhorses, and Victorian nosegays. Wearing Sunday clothes was quite restricting too because they had to be kept clean. All respectable little girls had special underwear for Sundays. Instead of her elasticated, fleecy-lined knickers, Emmie wore white cotton knickers that buttoned to her Liberty bodice. A front flap buttoned to the sides of the bodice and the back flap to the same buttons. Around the legs were needlework frills. Emmie wore two petticoats on Sundays – a plain, white cotton one, and a pretty, cream flannel one with scalloped edges. These were not new but passed on from a good customer. She had a velvet dress with a lace collar and over this was fastened her starched and frilled pinafore.

When Emmie tired of the scrapbooks, the walk to church was a relief. The people of Deep Pits Church were eager for their social life but worship was their first priority. Emmie attended church three times each Sunday. She was happy to go to church and Sunday school and looked forward to all the Christian festivals.

The Chapel Anniversary sermons were a momentous annual occasion for the village. A special tiered platform was erected over the stage for seating. The platform was almost as high as the ceiling; and how exhilarating it was to sit on the top step! Emmie, like all the other girls, was dressed in white. They were seated down the centre. The boys filled in the sides and the adult choir was below with the orchestra. Rousing hymns, of the kind for which Methodists are renowned, filled the chapel, and Emmie fixed her eyes dutifully on the conductor and his baton. She and her friends were encouraged to sing solos and recite from an early age. Emmie never forgot this first ordeal. She stood transfixed, concentrating on

Mr Buckland, who conducted her tenderly, mouthing the words to reassure her. Mr Ironside, the organist, played gently so the childish voice could be heard and the packed congregation was hushed, willing her to reach the end of her verse without any mishaps. There was a smiling murmur as she took a deep breath and sat down. Mr Buckland gave her a smile before turning to the next soloist. When this awesome moment of glory was over, Emmie relaxed. During the sermon her attention wandered, and she played with the scalloped edge of her best petticoat and admired the embroidery.

Then came a well-practised anthem or cantata by the enlarged choir and orchestra. Other local churches supported them on this special day. The congregation was bigger than usual, so full of family and friends that some people had to sit outside. A great swell of harmony arose and Frank Presley's gloriously deep voice contrasted with the sweetness of the sopranos. Emmie lost herself in the music. One day she would be in the choir too.

As the final grace was spoken the sun shone through the windows. The sun always shone on anniversary Sundays.

8. A Polite Visit

Emmie's paternal grandparents lived on Bernard Street in the Park District, where Hyde Park flats now stand. Row upon row of terraced houses stood almost on top of each other, looking down on the Midland Station. Grandad Evans's house was a strange, triangular shape, built where two rows of houses met at a right angle. Emmie believed that her gentle red-haired grandmother – whose maiden name had been Harriet Shannon – had Irish origins. She was a quiet lady, not very strong, who liked to stay at home. A little red crocheted shawl was always tied round her neck.

The house was very small and had no back door! Anyone needing the lavatory, which was outside at the back of the house, had a long walk. Leaving by the shop door at the front, they had to walk along the street and round the back of all the houses. Grandad Evans was a shoemaker by trade and the front room was a cobbler's shop. Very little accommodation was left for the family, yet Thomas (senior) and Harriet had raised four children within its walls. There was Emmie's father, 'young Thomas' and a daughter, Anna. Emmie never knew her Aunt Anna who had left home to become a dancer in London. No one seemed to speak about Anna. There was Frances who had married a Sheffield headteacher, Charles Furniss. They lived on Stafford Road with two grown-up children, also named Frances and Charles. Emmie did know them. She loved Aunty Frances who was a sweet-tempered invalid, but her cousin Frances had a very sharp tongue. Their household was rather Victorian. Another son was William who married Annie Bird. They had three children, William, Ernest and Phyllis. Phyllis was a little younger than Emmie and the two cousins were very fond of each other. Phyllis loved to come to tea with Emmie but she didn't live near so opportunities to play together were infrequent. Sometimes they wrote letters to each other and exchanged postcards.

Emmie loved writing letters and frequently ran out to post them in the letterboxes carried on the postal trams. A letter to Phyllis, posted in the evening, often arrived next morning and brought a quick and eager response.

One day, after school, her mother told Emmie that her cousin Frances had spoken to her when she had delivered the milk.

"She has invited you and Phyllis to go to tea and stay overnight."

Emmie put down her sandwich and considered. She thought of the severe Victorian atmosphere. She was nervous of her grown-up cousin Frances and she had never spent a night there. But if Phyllis was going to be there... It would be lovely to see Phyllis! In any case, she could hardly refuse.

On Friday night, Emily packed a bag for Emmie and showed her all its contents. Then she took Emmie on the tram to Stafford Road. Trams now ran up City Road nearly as far as the farmhouse. Emmie was first to arrive and kissed cousin Frances politely. Then she sat on a little stool near Aunty Frances who had a big tartan rug over her knees. While Emmie was searching for conversation, Phyllis arrived. The two little girls were happy and relieved to see each other. Cousin Frances wanted to know what they were learning at school and was pleased when they could recite their tables. Then, while cousin Frances made tea, Aunty Frances wanted to hear all about the farm. Both

Emmie and Phyllis enjoyed chatting about the animals. Then Uncle Charles came in with the roly-poly dog, Gyp. Amazingly, he found a penny in each of Gyp's ears, which he gave to the girls. He was a member of the Magic Circle and his tricks kept Emmie and Phyllis happy until teatime. They were actually enjoying themselves! They ate salad, jelly and cake very politely and helped to clear away the dishes. Aunty Frances showed them her music-box and there was time for a game of 'Ludo' before bed. Then, dressed in their long nightgowns, they climbed into a high double bed, covered in a big silk eiderdown. The curtains were drawn and it was very dark and a little scary but it was exciting too. They whispered to each other until they fell asleep.

Next morning, after breakfast, cousin Frances made sure that they were neat and tidy. She tied new ribbons in their hair.

"We're going into Sheffield to have your photographs taken," she told them. She intended this to be a big treat but the girls were in awe of the photographer's studio and even more of the camera, draped in black cloth. Emmie sat in a special chair and the photographer positioned Phyllis by her side. They both stared solemnly as the camera clicked. Astonished to realise it was over so quickly, they relaxed and enjoyed the rest of their morning in town. When their visit was over they thanked cousin Frances for having them. She told their parents graciously that they had behaved very well. A few weeks later the photograph arrived. In spite of their serious expressions it was a very charming picture.

31

9. SPROTBOROUGH

If Emmie had been apprehensive about staying with cousin Frances, she had no such doubts about staying with her relatives in Sprotborough. In fact these visits were highlights in her life. After being sold to the farm at Gildingwells, her grandfather, Walter, didn't return to live at Sprotborough and rarely spoke about the intervening years. But he did stay in contact with his family. His half-brothers and sisters were considered relations and Emmie loved to go there.

Careful planning preceded these outings and the milk round had to be re-organised. Thomas sometimes delivered it in the night. One visit stood out in Emmie's mind. The family set off very early in the morning in the pony and trap. The sun was rising and the birds were singing. This was a real day's holiday! It was a long journey and the pony was given frequent rests. When they were nearly there, the trap descended the steep winding hill to the wide river – so different from Deep Pits, Emmie could hardly contain her excitement.

Thomas always stopped the pony on the bridge so that they could admire the water rushing over the weir. Further along the bridge they paused again to look down on the many barges waiting to go through the canal lock. After this final rest, the pony plodded wearily up the other side into the village, and Emmie was glad to see there was a stable waiting for him. Uncle Joe rubbed him down and gave him fresh hay and water. The pony shared the stable with the Post Office horse. The family was made welcome too. Great-aunt Polly and Great-aunt Ada were unmarried. There were no children at the Post Office so they always made a fuss of Emmie. Her parents had to travel back the same day, but Emmie sometimes stayed for several days.

The Post Office cottage was small and the door was so low that Uncle Joe had to duck his head every time he passed through it. Emmie slept on a homemade box-like bed, tucked into an alcove. It was a converted shelf, very narrow, and Emmie slept stretched out. On Sundays she attended church with her aunts and was very impressed by the ancient building. In the evenings the cottage was cosy. The beams were very low and attached to them were glass walking sticks won at fairgrounds. The long glass sticks had been twisted into tight spirals and they were filled with 'hundreds and thousands'. These minute coloured sweets reflected in the glass and sparkled in the lamplight. Emmie stared at them as she drank her hot milk at bedtime.

Great-aunt Polly said, "You like those, don't you, Emmie?"

"They are so pretty, Aunt Polly," said Emmie.

"Well, one day one of them will be yours," said Aunt Polly. "Isn't that right, Ada?"

Aunt Ada nodded. "That's right, and we won't forget."

33

Emmie was thrilled. After that, every time she looked at them she wondered which one of them would be hers.

Emmie's aunts did some work for Lady Copley at Sprotborough Hall. In case Emmie should meet this important person while out walking with her aunts, she was washed and made presentable each time they ventured forth. Aunt Polly instructed her to step off the pavement to let the lady pass and Aunt Ada inspected her curtsey. Emmie was well versed in curtseying, thanks to Deep Pits amateur theatricals.

"You must remember to curtsey," Aunt Ada emphasised.

In her eagerness to please her aunts, Emmie curtsied to several ladies before meeting Lady Copley but when they did, at last, encounter the lady herself, Emmie remembered her manners. Lady Copley smiled and praised her behaviour, much to the gratification of her aunts.

Time always flew by when Emmie stayed at Sprotborough and, although she was always happy to return to Deep Pits, it was hard to say goodbye. She waved to Uncle Joe, Aunt Polly and Aunt Ada until they were out of sight. Sprotborough was her magical place.

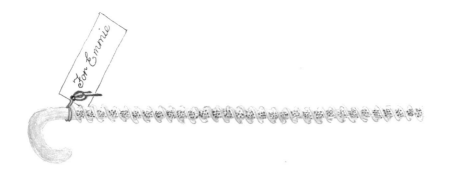

10. Work and Play

Thomas and Emily were never rich but they had more security than most. Times were hard and there was real poverty. Thomas's father had passed on his shoemaking and cobbling trade to his son, who was an apt pupil. Those who knew Young Thomas said that he worked hard all round the clock. He rose at dawn to harness the horse to fetch the milk – not just from the City Road farm, but also from much further afield and the big churns were heavy. Milk was delivered over a wide area and customers liked it early. During the day, he attended to his pigs and his other livestock. He always found time for his garden and greenhouse. Always in the afternoon, he worked in his workshop. His marriage certificate recorded that his father was a shoemaker and that he, 'Young Thomas', was a 'boot and shoe riveter'.

When he set up his own workshop at Don Terrace he was allowed to call himself a shoemaker. Photos from his courting days show him to be a well-dressed young man. Emmie thought her father looked very smart on Sundays, but on weekdays he wore an old brown coat-overall. One of his first jobs had been to train profoundly deaf men to make and repair shoes at a school in Sheffield. Frequently these men called at his workshop for advice and all kinds of help. He assisted them in filling in forms. Thomas used sign language fluently. Emmie learned some signs and the letters of the alphabet so that she could communicate a little.

Emmie loved to watch her father at work. He could throw a handful of nails into his mouth and position them between his teeth with his tongue. He spat them out rhythmically exactly where needed and tapped them in at lightning speed with the plain edge of a file. He could make designs with nails very quickly. Emmie was delighted to have roses under her shoes.

Journeys into Sheffield to the tannery were opportunities for Emmie to go with her father in the pony and trap. Emmie looked after the horse while he went inside. Her nose wrinkled as the strong odours drifted from within. Thomas selected large sheets of leather. Emmie liked the smell of those. They were stiff, like boards, and were not easy to fit into the trap. When out on these jaunts, Thomas sometimes took the opportunity to look at the local shoe shops. He stopped the trap and he and Emmie jumped down to gaze critically into the shop windows. He looked intently, sometimes muttering adverse comments or exclaiming, "That's a good piece of leather!" Emmie walked up and down with him. She noticed that, on these occasions, he always sang in an abstracted way in his absorption: "For the Lord God omnipotent reigneth. Hallelujah!" Then, this idle moment suddenly over, they were on their way home again.

Thomas had many special customers. One very lame lady came regularly for a built-up boot. All the shoes were made-to-measure. Emmie's mother worked hard too. Before she was married she had risen early to make breakfast for her father and brothers on the farm. She had also been in service at Richmond Hall. She was used to hard work. She delivered milk with Thomas and as the round grew they took on a teenage girl to help. Evelyn came to 'live-in' at the dairy. She settled in well and became 'one of the family'. She shared Emmie's bed. Emmie didn't mind. The two girls were very happy together. Emily was particularly glad of her help. It gave her more time for preparing food. A good cook, she made use of all available produce, pickling eggs, bottling fruit and turning sour cream into delicious cheese. She could pluck a chicken, skin a rabbit and make ice cream to sell in the dairy.

It was generally accepted that Mrs Evans 'kept a good table'. Watching people enjoying their food gave Emily great satisfaction. Family parties were good reasons for baking. At Christmas time, the Bell family had a grand get-together in the farmhouse. Emmie helped her mother to line a child's clean, zinc bath with spotless tea towels. Inside, they placed dozens of mince pies, butterfly buns, jam and lemon tarts and iced dainties. Emmie's aunts arrived early and added their own contributions. The bath was carried across the road and into the farmhouse. While the men inspected the cattle and farm machinery, the women organised cups and saucers. The big table was spread with a snowy white cloth and everything set ready for a feast.

Muddy boots had to be wiped before the men gathered round the fire to exchange news. The children ran about and were told, "Stop getting under my feet!"

At that stage, ten cousins joined in the Christmas fun but more would be born as the years passed. William's daughter, Doris, was nine years older than Emmie and was helping with the preparations. Her young brothers, William, Leonard and Jack, joined Emmie and Norah in a game of hide and seek. Walter's little boy, Walter, and Edie and Sam's only child, Joy, toddled about, tumbling down as they tried to follow the bigger children. Aunt Annie nursed baby Ronnie. The children grew noisier and confusion among all the Williams and Walters caused constant muddles. Emmie thought it silly to call children after their parents but, wisely, never said so.

At last, Grandad Bell called for some order and made sure that his wife was settled comfortably in her rocking-chair. All the grown-ups found a chair – some borrowed from the dairy – but most were dusted down after being relegated to the barn. The boys sat on a bench from Thomas's workshop and Emmie and Norah had small stools. Gossiping continued, but not so loudly as before. Ham sandwiches, pickled onions, pork pies and rich fruitcake disappeared in enormous quantities. It was a true Yorkshire high tea.

Norah was the daughter of Emily's sister, Ada. To Emmie, she was more like a sister than a cousin. Emmie loved all her cousins and her many friends but Norah was the one with whom she shared all her secrets. If Emily made a new dress for Emmie, she made one for Norah. So did Ada. The girls sat together wearing matching dresses and talking non-stop.

After tea the family played games. Old and young joined in. 'How green you are' was a favourite. The singing was deafening as the searcher grew nearer to the hidden thimble and faded to a whisper as the wrong direction was taken. Then everyone performed party pieces. Uncle Billy knew many long poems.

"Some were far too long and awfully sad," thought Emmie. So did Norah. They giggled and then tried to control themselves as their mothers frowned at them. Uncle Billy, by popular request, recited 'The Green Eye of the Little Yellow God'. They thought that was rather scary and huddled up together.

Cousin Doris played the piano. She was very pretty and fashionable. She played beautifully and with such ease that Emmie was impressed. Aunt Edie followed her on the piano while Uncle Sam nursed their little girl, Joy. She soon fell asleep on his knee. Edie was very jolly and played the piano 'by ear'. She had a great repertoire of music hall songs and everyone joined in singing. No doubt the re-filled glasses helped to put everyone in good voice. Outside, the farmhouse windows glowed in the lamplight and the flickering flames of the log fire. The singing changed from music hall songs to well-known carols. The old house was filled with warmth and laughter. Emmie and Norah, wrapped in the loving security of a large family, were storing up golden memories.

11. Learning the Hard Way

E mmie had been so impressed by her cousin Dot's prowess on the piano that she begged her parents to let her learn too. Emily and Thomas agreed and she became a pupil of Mrs Ryder. Emmie liked Mrs Ryder and considered the black velvet choker she wore round her neck to be very stylish. However, she soon realised that playing the piano was not to be mastered overnight and that daily practice was not always pleasant or easy. Her parents did not have a piano so Emmie went every evening to practise on the one in the farmhouse.

The farmhouse kitchen was warmed and lit by a big fire. Unfortunately the piano was not in there. It stood in the 'best' room that was reached by climbing six wide stone steps. Emmie liked to stroke the polished handrail as she went up the steps. The room at the top was long and dark with a window looking out on to City Road. The piano stood beneath this window, and in winter Emmie found it an eerie place away from the light and warmth of the fire. A candle burned on the brackets on each side of the piano. On the wall behind her hung a large clock. On dark nights, when local people were passing the farmhouse, which jutted out into City Road, they frequently pressed their faces to the window hoping to read the time. Emmie, already nervous and struggling with an overactive imagination, was convinced at first that these were ghosts. Often she let out a small scream but no one noticed. Even when she understood the faces at the window, she found it alarming. The windowpane was loose. It rattled and let in a draught that blew the candles out. Grandma Bell was stone deaf and couldn't hear Emmie shouting. Occasionally Uncle Walter, who worked on the farm, came to encourage her but he couldn't play the piano. It was a lonely task.

Then Emmie's school friend, Kathleen, started dancing lessons and showed Emmie steps at playtime. How Emmie longed to dance! Her mother said that Emmie had made her choice and must persevere with her piano lessons. So, while her fingers stumbled over the notes, Emmie complained, "I want to learn to dance! I want to learn to dance!" But there was no one to hear and Emmie never dreamed how much pleasure her piano playing would eventually bring her and how useful it would be. Secretly she thought her parents were very strict. So did her friends. Some of them asked if her mother was a teacher. Emmie was horrified! She loved her parents deeply and considered teachers in general to be absolute harridans.

Sitting at the table one evening, she related, with a mixture of delight and horror, an incident that had taken place at school that day.

"You know the really awful teacher I told you about," she began. Thomas and Emily smiled at each other. "You know, the one who writes numbers all over the blackboard with coloured chalks and then asks hard questions?"

"Yes, you have mentioned her," said Emily.

"Well, today," Emmie continued, "she asked Dolly Richardson a really difficult question and Dolly couldn't answer. So she did what she always does. She rushed down to the back of the classroom, grabbed Dolly by her hair and ran her to the blackboard. Everybody was waiting to see what would happen because the last time she did that to Dolly, Dolly said she would run home next time."

"So what did happen?" asked Emily.

"Well," said Emmie, again with great emphasis, "well, the teacher held Dolly's hair very tightly and bumped her nose all over the blackboard. She kept saying, 'Now – get – this – into – your – head!' When she stopped, Dolly's nose was bright red, her face was covered in coloured chalk, and Dolly was crying. 'Now sit down!' Miss Rudd shouted but Dolly ran out of the classroom."

"So what happened then?" asked Thomas.

"Miss Rudd looked very cross and said it was playtime so we all went out to play. But – this is the best bit," said Emmie, "– after play we were all writing and the classroom door opened. Dolly's mother came in. Her hair was in curlers. She was so angry! She grabbed Miss Rudd by the hair and banged her nose on the blackboard! She really rubbed her face in the coloured chalk. Then she let Miss Rudd go and stormed off. She slammed the door hard! Miss Rudd went out too and we all began to laugh. Then the headteacher came in and we all went quiet."

Thomas and Emily exchanged glances and their eyes twinkled.

"That sounds like Alice Richardson," commented Thomas. He looked at Emmie and said, "Make sure you keep your nose clean."

Emmie did try to keep her nose clean and she worked very hard at school. Her main motivation was fear. The almost daily rapping of her knuckles with a ruler resulted in beautiful handwriting. Emmie was determined to achieve good marks. Last year she had been pleased with her report. She showed it to her father with pride because she was second in the class. Her father was not pleased. He looked at the marks and said, "You have no need to be pleased with yourself. You can do much better than this." Her legs had been smacked hard. So Emmie was anxious to do better and waited for her report with apprehension. This year she was top of the class and breathed a sigh of relief when her father was satisfied.

"Well done!" he said.

12. Late for School!

Emily was sitting by the fire pegging a rug. The clean hessian was spread over her knee. Emmie was cutting strives from old clothes and dropping them into a box. As she snipped away at the old navy coat, she was thinking again about her teachers.

"Were they strict when you went to school, Mum?" she asked.

"We went to a strange school," Emily told her. "We had to pay fourpence a week. It was a long, low building that was almost tumbling down. We learned to write on slates, and when it rained they had to go back on the roof." She laughed at the utter disbelief on Emmie's face. "It's quite true. There were two classes. The headmaster taught the boys and his daughter taught the girls. If she was cross with us and raised her voice, he would come to the door and tell her that she must not shout at the young ladies."

So school was not so bad for the girls!

Emily continued. "He was not so soft with the boys. When two boys misbehaved he fetched them out in front of the class. One boy had to bend over and the other was given a cane. Then the headmaster would say, 'Lay into him because he is going to do the same to you!'." Emmie looked shocked. "Education was not considered so important then," Emily said. "It was not unusual for a parent to request that their child ran errands. The headmaster would say, 'Billy, your mother wants a pound of potatoes. Be quick now. She wants them for your father's dinner' and the boy would run out of school."

Emmie was astonished. "Did you all like school?" she asked.

"I was happy enough at school," her mother said. "My brother Billy did well at school. Walter was ready to leave. He liked to be with Dad on the farm. My sisters liked school – except for Nellie – you know... the one who died. Nellie was very nervous. She could never remember which was 'm' and which was 'n'. She used to whisper to me, 'two legs or three'?"

Emmie laughed. "But she learned to read and write, didn't she?"

"Oh yes," Emily said. "The only one who didn't learn was Florrie. She wouldn't go to school."

"Aunt Florrie was always different," said Emmie. "Aunt Edie told me she once fell down a well!"

Emily chuckled. "Florrie was lucky! She always wore more clothes than anyone else so when she fell, she stuck halfway down. She screamed so loudly you could have heard her at the Manor Top!"

Emmie was still thinking about school.

"My goodness! Fancy letting children run errands in school time! They wouldn't let us out of school. We daren't even be late."

$$* \quad * \quad * \quad * \quad *$$

Emmie was usually in plenty of time for school. She and Joe were accustomed to their long walk, which was full of familiar sights and sounds. They often waved to Emmie's Uncle Walter setting out on the coal cart. This cart was used for fetching coal but it was a general-purpose farm cart. Behind the Travellers Rest were allotments and as they passed, they met people carrying spades or vegetables. Emmie had an observant eye and remembered people. The children always said "Hello". As they walked along, they imagined what their neighbours' day held in store. They had the natural curiosity that comes from living in a closely-knit community. Sometimes their chatter subsided as they reached the cemetery gates. A sad cluster of people, a woman carrying a small white bundle, was a frequent sight and one that needed no explanation. Infant mortality was very high. But children are very resilient and Emmie and Joe felt their spirits lift as they reached the last section of the cemetery wall. When shuttlecock and battledore was in fashion they ran down the hill, trailing their battledores against the railings, enjoying the rhythmic clattering. When this ended, the school gates lay ahead.

But one day the children were late for school. Emmie, Joe and Nellie wanted to run, but Jessie's little legs could not keep up. The sight of Emmie's Grandad

43

approaching with his horse and high-sided cart filled them with hope. They pleaded for a lift. Grandad stopped cheerily. Little Jessie was almost thrown into the cart and the others scrambled hastily up the sides. Only as they tumbled into the cart did they realise that Grandad's errand was muck-spreading! Their boots squelched in a potent collection from hen-run, pig-sty, cowshed, and stable. The smell should have told them but they had only had one thought in their heads.

"Oh, Grandad!" cried Emmie, "Why didn't you tell us?"

"That will teach you to set off for school in time," said Grandad, mightily amused by their discomfiture.

They jumped down and went to face the wrath of their teachers. The teacher on duty gazed on them with distaste and made them leave their boots at the door. They were sent to wash. Even then a strong odour hung around them, causing their classmates much mirth. Behind the teacher's back, noses were held, eyes were crossed and hands fanned the air. When school was over, they faced further admonishment at home. It was some time before Emmie forgave Grandad.

13. Keeping Pigs

Thankfully for Emmie, school was only part of her life. She was expected to help at home but there was still time to play. Among her playmates was Mary Battams who lived in the same row of houses.

Mary was four years younger than Emmie but the age gap didn't seem to matter. They were both very imaginative and created all kinds of games. Sometimes Mary's older brother, Branson, joined in their games and occasionally their small sister, Lily, was included. Mary sometimes had to keep an eye on Lily, who was constantly in mischief. Like Emmie's father, their father kept pigs.

One day Lily had been found sitting in the pig trough. The pigs had eaten all the buttons from her coat! Mary's mother was not pleased. Nor was she on another occasion. Mary told Emmie the story as they sat in Grandad's barn. Mrs Battams had planned to take the children out and had dressed Lily first. That was a mistake! Lily was exceedingly pretty with rosy cheeks and white-blonde hair. She looked a picture in a shantung cream silk dress and a big bow in her hair. While the others were being dressed, Lily had toddled up the garden path and fallen into the pig slurry, which had been emptied at the top of the garden. She was covered from top to toe with slime when she was found.

"She smelled awful!" laughed Mary, wrinkling her nose at the memory.

"Whatever did your mother do?" asked Emmie.

"She stood her in the yard and poured water all over her. Then she stripped her clothes off. Lily howled the place down! Then mum finished her off inside." Both girls laughed. "We stayed at home," concluded Mary.

One thing that Emmie and Mary both hated was pig-killing day. Their fathers often hired the pig-killing man on the same day. Usually Mary's parents made sure that their children were elsewhere during these proceedings. Emmie didn't want to stay but was pressed to do so by some of the other children.

"If you stay, Emmie, your father will give you the pig's bladder," they pleaded.

The bladder was a real prize. Washed and blown up it became a football. The big boys in Deep Pits Yard wanted it too so there was competition. Emmie stayed, stuffing her fingers into her ears and closing her eyes until the pig had stopped screaming.

Afterwards the pig was laid on a trestle table. Buckets of scalding water were poured over it and the man shaved off all the bristles. Then it was hung from a big hook in the kitchen with a bowl beneath. A stick held its legs apart. Emmie's mother and Mary's mother were very busy at this stage. The fat was cut into cubes and salted. The cubes were put into the oven to make pork scratchings. More fat was poured into crocks to make lard. Then the pork was cut into handy joints. The head was made into brawn, the tongue cooked and pressed. All the small, lean pieces were made into pork pies with hand-raised hot-water pastry. The pies were delicious and the smell in their kitchens was mouthwatering. Everyone agreed that 'nothing is wasted on a pig but its whistle'.

Eventually, Emmie's father would hang a large side of ham from the ceiling at the top of the stairs. The local doctor, a good friend, called sometimes and said, "That's a fine side of ham, Evans." He never went away empty-handed.

Thomas fed his pigs well and believed he could feed a pig to exact requirements of lean, fat or streaky. He stored his pork in a huge box of salt in the attic. Over one winter the salt corroded the bottom of the box. No one noticed until long cracks appeared in the bedroom ceiling! Disaster was imminent.

Thomas had repairs made immediately. The house was rented from the Duke of Norfolk and was not their own. Consequences could have been serious and the matter was hushed up.

Emmie and Mary were always sad when the pigs had to be killed but accepted it as a part of their lives. There was no doubt that the bacon sandwiches and pork pies were scrumptious. Their parents, who had all known what it was to be hungry, were grateful for the opportunity to keep pigs.

They always said, "It keeps the wolf from the door."

14. A Surprise

"Emmie, have a quick wash. We're going on the tram to Aunty Ada's."
Emmie, just home from school, was astonished, but realised it was not the time to be asking questions and obeyed. When they were seated on the tram her mother explained.

"Our Ada is not very well so we're going to stay the night. You'll have to sleep with Norah." Emmie's face lit up at spending the night with Norah but she remembered Aunty Ada.

"Poor Aunty," she said. "Is that why we have so many bags?"

"Yes," said Emily. "We need our nightclothes. I've made a meat and potato pie and a treacle tart. Your father has Evelyn to help him. Uncle Ted needs us to help him because he has to look after the shop."

Aunty Ada was in bed when Emmie and her mother arrived at the grocer's shop. Emily went straight up to see her sister. Uncle Ted gave the girls an apple each and they sat on the back step together.

"What's wrong with your Mam?" asked Emmie.

"I don't know," replied Norah, "but she seems to have some bad tummy ache."

Norah fetched her skipping rope and they tried some of the fancy skipping Emmie had been learning at Girls Brigade.

"Sometimes we skip to music," she told Norah. They tried singing but were soon puffed out. "You're better than I am!" Emmie said.

Emily called them for dinner and the pie and the treacle tart were eaten with gusto by the girls but Uncle Ted didn't seem hungry. He closed the shop early and went to sit with Ada. Emily went up to the attic bedroom to see Emmie and Norah tucked in and reminded them that Norah's mother was not well.

"She needs peace and quiet so be extra good," said Emily as she left them.

The girls looked up at the stars through the skylight window and whispered for a while, but skipping had tired them and they were soon asleep. Emmie was dreaming that she was having a tug-of-war with Jack. The dog was pulling and towsing the end of her skipping rope. Abruptly, he let go and Emmie was falling backwards. Her eyes opened. "Where am I?" she thought, then realised that her mother had been shaking her. Norah was sitting up, rubbing her eyes. Was the house on fire?

"Listen!" said Emily. "There's something special for you to see in the kitchen. Come downstairs quietly."

Sleepy and puzzled, the girls followed Emily into the lamp-lit kitchen. A big fire burned in the grate. A lady they did not know was there with her back to them. She turned and placed a bundle into Emily's arms.

"If you're alright," she said to Emily, "I'll go back to your sister." Then she smiled at the girls. "Come and see your fine, new brother!"

Emmie and Norah were mystified. Their eyes grew large with astonishment as Emily unwrapped the bundle a little and they saw a small, red face and a damp, downy head.

"He's your brother, Norah," Emily said.

"Does Mam know?" asked Norah.

Like most children, she and Emmie were innocent of the facts of life. Even Emmie, used to animals on the farm, had given little thought to human reproduction

and it was not something that was discussed in front of children.

"Of course she does," said Emily. "She's just given birth to him. So now she needs to rest."

No more thought was given to Norah's mother. Their full attention was devoted to the baby.

"He's just going to have his first bath. Here, sit in the big chair and hold your new brother, Norah, while I fill the bowl."

Emily waited while Norah generously made room for Emily by her side. When they were squeezed into the big chair, Emily placed the baby on Norah's knee. She held him with awe and carefulness. Sheer joy left them wordless. Emmie peeped under the sheet and found the baby's toes. His eyes were shut tightly. Emily filled an enamel bowl and laid out some cotton wool. Two towels were already warming on the fireguard, and on the line beneath the mantelpiece hung a baby's vest, a nightgown and nappies. Emily took the baby on to her knee and opened the cotton sheet that wrapped him. Immediately he began to cry, little red fists and knees thrusting angrily. Emmie and Norah sat on the edge of the chair, amazed to hear such a tiny scrap making such a loud noise.

"Hush! Hush!" crooned Emily and wrapped him snugly in a towel. The baby calmed a little and Emily tucked him under one arm, cradling his head with one hand. Holding his head over the bowl, she dipped the cotton wool into the warm water and bathed his head. Then she patted him dry with the other towel. She used a fresh piece of cotton wool to clean each eye, another for his nose and another for his mouth. Suddenly his eyes opened and both little girls were charmed. His eyes seemed too big for his face. He was beautiful! Spellbound, they watched as Emily cleaned every part of him. She told them how important it was to dry all the little creases in his elbows and knees. Then, with more cotton wool she powdered the baby. The scent of a clean, powdered baby filled the kitchen. Then Emily wrapped a clean binder round and round his tummy. The girls took turns to pass the tiny clothes. The baby objected to the vest but Emily's well-practised hands soon had it over his head. She pinned on a smooth muslin nappy and then rolled him in a towelling nappy that covered his tiny toes. Once dressed in a flannel nightgown, Emily laid him, face down, across her knee for a moment while she tied the strings of his nightgown loosely so they would not press into him. A knitted matinee coat was buttoned round him and he was wrapped in a white crocheted shawl. Only his tiny face peeped out.

"What is his name?" asked Norah.

"Your Mam wants to christen him Edward like your father," Emily told her, "but he'll be Teddy for short."

Then she stood up with Teddy in her arms. "You can give him a gentle kiss on his head, and then he's going to have some milk from his mother." Light dawned on Emmie as visions of suckling piglets, calves and kittens came into her mind. She and Norah gave him the lightest of kisses and he was taken upstairs.

Emily came back with a delighted smile. Mother and baby were doing well. She gave the girls a mug of hot milk and a biscuit.

"Fancy! Having a picnic in the middle of the night!" said Norah as they toasted their toes and watched the flames curling up the fire back.

"You are lucky having a brother, Norah," said Emmie wistfully.

"Well you can share him – really you can!" insisted Norah. Then Emily sent them back to bed.

The next day Emmie related the events of that exciting night to Grandma Bell.

"And Norah says I can share him!" she finished.

Emmie did share Norah's little brother. After that wonderful night she always felt that, in a very special way, Teddy belonged to her.

15. 'An Unsuitable Pet'

When Emmie had recovered from rheumatic fever, the local doctor had warned them that there could be setbacks.

"Rheumatic fever has lasting effects. She will be vulnerable to infections and you must always be on your guard," he told them. Naturally, Emmie's parents watched over her carefully and were concerned because, from time to time, she seemed to lose her appetite. Thomas, believing goat's milk to be nourishing, purchased both a nanny and a billy-goat. Unfortunately, Emmie could not stomach goat's milk so the nanny was sold. The billy-goat was kept because Emmie adored him. He had a shining, silky black coat and Emmie called him Black Billy. Like most billy-goats he was temperamental, but he loved Emmie and followed her round the field, returning her adoration.

One day, Black Billy's devotion to Emmie caused a lot of bother. Emmie blamed the big boys from Deep Pits Yard. They had noticed how the goat trotted behind Emmie and thought it would be funny to release him and see what happened. He was tethered by a long rope. The boys watched Emmie depart for school, and then waited until she was past the Traveller's Rest before untying the rope from the stake. They held on to the rope tightly and with Black Billy dancing around madly, they took him along the road. Black Billy saw his beloved Emmie ahead of him and pulled on the rope. As Emmie disappeared through the school gates, they let go of the rope and the goat was gone in a flash. He followed Emmie into the hall where all the children were assembling and created a wonderful disturbance. Children screamed, children chased and the teacher demanded, "Whose goat is this?"

Emmie confessed that the goat belonged to her. She calmed him down and suggested timorously that she should take him home. The teacher was shocked.

"A goat is a most unsuitable pet for a little girl!" she exclaimed. "It would be most dangerous for you to take him home. You are not strong enough to hold on to him." Emmie tried to explain that Black Billy would simply follow her back to the farm but the teacher would not listen. She sent a message to the boys' department, asking for two big boys to take the goat home. The same boys, having achieved their aim, smirked at Emmie and escaped school for most of the morning.

The goat had left a smelly souvenir in the school hall. The caretaker cleared this away but a goat's smell is very persistent. It reeked for days.

The boys allowed some time to pass before repeating their misdeed. After the third time Emmie came home to find that Black Billy had been sold. Other complaints had been made. Black Billy had eaten several newly planted hedges and some washing from a clothes-line.

Emmie grieved for him and one evening, riding through Intake in the trap, she was sure she saw him pulling a cart. A little boy was riding in it while his father walked alongside. Emmie was regretful but pleased to see that someone was caring for Black Billy. She remembered him with great affection and she knew just how the little girl in the nursery rhyme *Mary had a little lamb* had felt.

16. NIGHT ANGELS AND CHAMBER POTS

Emmie's family considered themselves very fortunate because every house in Don Terrace had its own lavatory and they did not have to share with neighbours. These outside buildings were brick-built and situated across the yard, hygienically away from the houses. The doorsteps, like the house steps, were regularly scrubbed and donkey-stoned to give them a clean and gleaming appearance. Emmie's mother took a pride in keeping the place spotless. The lavatory seat was of the old-fashioned sort, a long board with one hole. Some families had more accommodation with two, or even three, holes. To prevent any unpleasant smells, ashes were scooped from a bucket and tipped into the lavatory after use. The long brick walls behind the lavatories had wooden flaps through which the contents could be emptied. The 'night angels' who visited during the night and shovelled the contents into horse-drawn wagons did this unpleasant task.

On long summer days, visits to the outside lavatory were no problem but dark, winter evenings were another matter. Emmie's imagination played tricks and she was frightened.

Her mother used to say, "Sing Emmie! You'll be alright if you sing." Emmie didn't like the dark. They now had gaslights in the house but not in the lavatory. Occasionally, her mother stood a candle in the corner of the long board seat and warned Emmie to be extra careful. On a dark night, shivering in her nightgown, Emmie accidentally caught the candle and it fell into the hole. Instantly, flames shot out of the lavatory! Emmie was horrified and flattened herself against the lavatory door, holding her breath. To her relief the flames subsided, and a very shaken little girl ran through the dark to her parents. The candle flame had ignited methane gas.

When the summer holidays came, Nellie Jeffcock, the oldest child in the yard and accepted leader, gathered her followers together. She was looking unusually neat and tidy and she gave them firm instructions.

54

"Go and wash your hands and faces. Comb your hair and come back to me," she commanded them. Five minutes later Joe, Emmie and Jessie returned for inspection. Nellie surveyed them and was satisfied. She carried a bag containing a large dandelion and burdock bottle of cold tea. "If anyone takes it from us they will be disappointed," she commented, adding, "I am taking you on a long walk. You must remember your manners."

Nellie led them up the hill, over the Manor Top, and down to Intake. By this time the bottle was almost empty and Jessie was clamouring for the lavatory.

Nellie stopped by a gateway and announced triumphantly, "Here we are! Remember your manners," she reminded them, and walked up the path to knock on the door. A lady answered, smiling pleasantly. "Please," asked Nellie. "We've walked a long way and we need the lavatory. Please could we go to your lavatory?"

The lady, who must have been enjoying fame and admiration, invited them in one at a time.

Nellie went first and, as she came out, she whispered to them, "You have to pull the chain." The children were mystified. What chain? Feeling quite nervous, Emmie went in next. She stared at the shining white ceramic lavatory. She thought it looked like an enormous jug. There was the chain! She pulled it tentatively. A little water ran from the rim of the white lavatory. She pulled it again and there was a tremendous gush of water! Would it flood over the sides? To her great relief, it swirled away, leaving the lavatory fresh and clean. Then she hurried back to the others. When they had all witnessed this amazing inside lavatory, they thanked the lady politely and set off for home, highly impressed. Nellie was complimented on this educational excursion.

*　*　*　*　*

Emmie sometimes slept at the farmhouse, sharing a bed with her Aunty Florrie. Aunty Florrie was the eccentric one of the Bell sisters. She had been christened Florice but this beautiful and unusual name had been shortened to Florrie or Flo. Considered to be 'a bit behind the door' by her family, Florrie could be surprisingly sharp-witted. Her brothers and sisters spoke well, with little local dialect or slang, perhaps because their father originated from Retford, but Florrie spoke differently. Most of her sentences began with 'Sithee!' and were delivered at top speed.

Emmie loved her kind and funny aunt. Sleeping with Aunty Florrie was always entertaining. Aunty Florrie squirrelled her sweets away in the old blanket chest and frequently woke Emmie to offer her a 'spice'. Emmie was sure that mice lived in the blanket chest and was dubious about these sticky offerings. Not wanting to hurt Aunty Florrie's feelings, she would murmur "Thank you", and suck her sweet obediently and sleepily.

Beneath the beds were the chamberpots. Almost every household used them. The process of 'emptying the slops' was an accepted chore and one mainly considered to be a girl's job. Emmie had to do it and learned to carry the bucket carefully.

One never-to-be-forgotten morning, Emmie was awakened by Aunty Florrie, who was kneeling on the blanket chest, leaning out of the window. She was quivering with excitement and anxiety.

"Sithee, Emmie, come and look!"

Emmie scrambled up beside her and they both stared down into the stack yard. Emmie's grandfather and Uncle Walter were trying to calm a large bull. It was a difficult and dangerous task. The bull had no intention of being directed into the field and turned this way and that, pawing the ground with an angry hoof and lowering his head threateningly. Aunty Florrie and Emmie watched fearfully. Grandad Bell had a stick through the ring on the bull's nose and was trying to steady the beast. The bull objected and backed into

56

Walter, crushing him against the horse trough that stood directly beneath the window.

"Me poor brother!" gasped Aunty Florrie. "Sithee, Emmie, pass me that bucket o' slops."

Emmie responded as quickly as possible, trying not to spill any. Aunty Florrie stood on the blanket chest and took aim at the bull. At that moment the bull kicked out, toppling Walter into the murky water of the horse trough. As he struggled to his feet, Aunty Florrie swung the bucket, which slipped from her hands, landed on Walter and emptied its contents over his head. Back he fell into the horse trough. Completely drenched and spluttering through the stinking effluent, he uttered some extremely undesirable words!

17. SUMMERTIME

During the summer holidays, Emmie and her friends were free to roam the countryside. Even when houses bordered most of City Road as far as Don Terrace, and the tram route reached the farmhouse, the people of Deep Pits felt they lived in the country. Behind the houses, on each side of the road, fields spread for miles. The corn still waved where vast housing estates now stand. Manor Lane, Spring Lane, Wulfric Road and Windy House Lane were all true country lanes. The children could walk through fields all the way to Bowden Woods where the Parkway now runs into Sheffield.

Most of the time, the children were content to play nearer home. Emmie's Grandad Bell never seemed to mind their playing round the farm. The duck pond was always an attraction. Trees grew round the pond and the cows drank there. The children caught sticklebacks, newts and frogs. Mary Battams, convinced that the dragonflies were fairies, fell in trying to catch them. Her brother, Branson, pulled her out and tried to dry her with dock leaves. They were both in trouble.

"Why weren't you watching your little sister?" scolded their mother. "Look at your clothes!" she said crossly to Mary, and gave her a none-too-gentle scrubbing in the tin bath. The next day poor Mrs Battams regretted her impatience when Mary was taken to Lodge Moor Hospital with scarlet fever. The pond water was considered to be the cause of her infection. Happily, Mary recovered from her illness and, quite undeterred by this experience, continued to play with Emmie around the farm. Together they climbed over the five-barred gate opposite their homes and ran down the sloping field to the brook where a willow tree hung over the stream. They spent many happy, dream-filled hours hidden in the tree among the leaves. The willow tree was split, forming a ledge from which, with daring, the stream could be leapt.

At one end of Farmer Bell's barn was a platform, ideal for concerts. The children made and sold tickets for one of their more serious efforts.

"What shall we do with the money?" asked Mary.

"Shall we give it to the Gloops Club?" suggested Emmie.

Everyone was in favour of this. Gloops was a cartoon character that appeared daily in the Star newspaper. The Gloops Club raised money for good causes. The tickets cost a halfpenny for children and a penny for adults. Emmie, Lily Hanson, Joe, Jessie, Mary and Lily Battams decorated their woolly hats with feathers from the chicken runs for the concert. They performed a short play about a poem they had learned at school. One behind the other they marched up and down the stage chanting:

> *Up the airy mountain,*
> *Down the rushy glen,*
> *We dare not go a-hunting*
> *For fear of little men.*

Unfortunately, the play was too short and the audience, mainly local children, rebelled and demanded a refund. So the Gloops Club did not benefit from this drama. Not disheartened for long, Emmie and her friends found other things to do. They practised acrobatics up the garden ready for the next show. Mary's little sister was becoming quite agile, and mastered handstands. She did a handstand to the newly painted lavatory door and her feet stuck to the paint. Her yells brought her mother rushing to the rescue. Her shoes were cleaned with turpentine, but the lavatory door was decorated with two footprints for years to come.

*   *   *   *   *

Not many children had holidays and Emmie's parents could not leave the milk round. Emmie was excited when Grandad Evans came to say he had plans to take her out for a day.

"Where are we going, Grandad?" she asked.

"Out into Derbyshire," he replied. "The charabanc is going to Matlock. There are some very high rocks there and a river. We'll take a towel. There might be a chance for a paddle."

Emmie hoped that it would be a fine day but the weather did not look very promising. Nevertheless their spirits were high as they climbed up the steps and through the doors nearest to their seats. Everyone was wrapped up very warmly because the charabanc was 'open-top'. On the door was written 'Sedgewicks of Intake, licensed to carry 32'. More than forty people climbed aboard for this big adventure! The smart, chain-driven 'chara' was loaded with people. A photograph was taken and showed Emmie, wearing a big hat, smiling delightedly from behind her grandfather. His daughter, Frances, with her daughter, Frances, sat proudly in the front seats. Emmie thought her grown-up cousin looked very fashionable. Wearing a black outfit, which matched her large, dark eyes, young Frances cut a very dramatic figure.

When the driver had reassured himself that all his passengers were settled, they waved to those left behind and settled back to make the most of their day. The speed amazed Emmie, and the cold air rushed by her in a most exhilarating way. She pulled her hat down over her ears but it threatened to blow away.

She tapped Grandad on his shoulder. "Grandad, I'm losing my hat!"

Kind old Grandad gave her his scarf. "Tie this round it," he said.

The lady sitting next to her laid the scarf over Emmie's hat and tied it under her chin. Now, with her hat secure and her ears warm, Emmie could relax and enjoy the journey. She thought the scenery was splendid and wondered at the miles and miles of stone walls. Sometimes they passed a herd of cows and Emmie surveyed them with particular interest. She must tell Grandad Bell about them.

Matlock was magnificent. Never could Emmie have imagined the Heights of Abraham. The weather was warm enough for the promised paddle and the children squealed at the cold river water. Cousin Frances had brought a picnic to share and Emmie had a wonderful day. Everyone was counted back on to the charabanc at the end of the day and there was some consternation when one family was missing. A great shout went up when they eventually came into view. They were well and truly scolded as they found their places.

"Come on, we're all waiting!"

"What time do you call this?"

"We nearly went without you!"

Darkness fell as they journeyed home and rain began to fall. Emmie, expecting to be soaked, was surprised to find that the charabanc had a roof! At home, chatting to her parents over her supper, Emmie told them, "It began to rain and the driver stopped. A wooden shed came over our heads!"

Grandad had enjoyed taking Emmie out for the day and he promised to take her again.

"Next time," he said, "we'll have a proper holiday and we'll go to the seaside."

A hot spell in late summer prompted Farmer Bell to start the haymaking. He and his two sons, William and Walter, sharpened their scythes and worked their way rhythmically across the fields, casting swathes of sweet-smelling grass and clover in long, curving patterns. Each stroke of the scythe laid a fan of hay on the ground. Insects rose at their approach. Garden tiger-moths, scarlet underwings glowing, disturbed from their daytime sleep, mingled with midges and honey bees. Emmie, on the edge of the field, admired the metallic flash of the Six-spot Burnet moths with their graceful antennae and their bright red spots. She didn't know their names but all living creatures appealed to her. On this hot morning she observed the miniature world around her in absorbed solitude. Golden ragwort flowers grew close by and Emmie noticed brightly coloured caterpillars winding round the leaves and stems. They were Cinnabars, yellow, with black bands.

"Like football jerseys," thought Emmie.

The hot weather continued and Farmer Bell was very grateful. He and his sons were able to turn the hay. They worked almost at walking speed, tossing the hay deftly with their forks in a way that looked easy but was the result of years of practice. Making the haycocks followed and this, too, looked deceptively easy as the men strode along heaping the swathes of sweet-smelling hay into rounded domes. Emmie and Norah were kept busy on these hot days carrying heavy stone jars of cider across the fields. The men were glad to see them. It was thirsty work! By the time the fields were spread with haycocks, Farmer Bell and his sons were weary and ready to rest.

Eventually, on the last day of the summer holidays, the hay was gathered in. Every available horse and wagon was brought into use. Large wooden frames were laid over the bodies of the carts and fitted firmly to extend carrying capacity. At each end of the frames gate-like structures, known locally as gormers, were slotted in vertically to safely increase the height of the loads. Every one joined in to help, including the children. Emmie and her friends loved to be out in the fields carrying great armfuls of hay, but haymaking was not a game and Farmer Bell was ready to send them home if they were 'in the way'. All the children hoped for a ride on the haycart, and there was a cheer when they were allowed to scramble up on to the final load. Emmie climbed up cautiously, having been warned not to let some well-meaning labourer throw her up on to the wagon in case she should land on a pitchfork or some other tool carelessly thrust into the hay. She already bore a white scar above her knee, having fallen on a scythe. Once aloft, the children clung to each other and sang as the horses pulled their loads along the lanes and into the stack yard. There the men had more skilled work, building haystacks that would not lean over or collapse. Haystacks needed ventilation. It was not unusual for haystacks to overheat and burst into flames.

The sun was sinking when the children, glowing after their day in the fresh air, returned to their homes and their beds. Next day, in school, they were fidgety. They scratched at insect bites and found grass seeds in their socks. The scolding of their teachers had little effect. Nothing could detract from that glorious day making hay while the sun shone!

18. Around the Year

Soon after her day out with Grandad Evans, the autumn term began. Emmie knew that this year her class would be going to the Park Baths for swimming lessons. She looked forward to these sessions with excitement. On their first visit, she and Lily Hanson shared one of the tiny cubicles that lined each side of the pool. All the girls came out rather self-consciously and inclined to giggle, but quietened down and gave full attention as they were instructed strictly 'to walk and not run along the edges of the pool'. Once in the water, they learned how to move their arms and legs for the breaststroke.

Then the instructor took each girl for a trial swim. Soon it was Emmie's turn. The instructor held a long pole over the water and Emmie found herself suspended from it by a loop of rope that went round her tummy. The instructor walked along and she had to move her arms and legs. Several times the pole was lowered carelessly as the instructor was distracted, and Emmie sank beneath the water and came up spluttering. Fortunately, she had been to the baths with her mother and was almost swimming. Spurred on by this unpleasant experience, Emmie learned to swim very quickly!

Swimming was going well but then a problem arose. The teacher was leading the girls along the road to the baths when an old man with a fierce expression stopped his horse, looked down from the trap and scrutinised the line of girls. The teacher stopped, deferentially recognising the local doctor. The old man's fiery gaze singled out Emmie. She knew him well. So did most of the girls.

"Emmie Evans! You should not be swimming. I've told your parents that rheumatic fever has lasting effects. Back to school!"

The teacher could hardly flout the doctor's advice so she spoke kindly to Emmie.

"Go back to the head teacher's room and tell Miss Corner what has happened. She will give you some work to do."

Emmie set off back to school reluctantly. Dr. Beecher flicked his reins and the horse trotted on.

That night Emmie complained bitterly to her parents. "Miss Corner was kind and she gave me some of her own books to read but I want to go swimming. Anyway, there's nothing wrong with me. I'm perfectly alright!"

Emmie's parents knew there was some truth in what the old doctor had said but they did not want Emmie treated as an invalid. They wanted her to swim. The teacher wanted Emmie to swim and Emmie wanted to swim. It was decided to risk the doctor's wrath. The journey to the baths became one of subterfuge. The doctor often drove along the road and there was a general conspiracy to hide Emmie. Concealing her added a spice of adventure to the children's' walk that Emmie did not share.

"The doctor's coming!" brought the class to a halt, and the teacher gathered them together as Emmie ducked down behind a wall or hid under a hedge.

"I'll stand in front of you," volunteered several children enthusiastically. Emmie crouched down, convinced that her protectors would draw attention to her. She held her breath as she heard the horse's hooves slow down and speed up again.

"You can come out again! He's gone now," the children reassured and, full of relief, Emmie breathed again. Occasionally there was no hiding place and then the game was up. "Back to school!"

Dr. Beecher was well-liked and respected in spite of his brusque manner. Patients visiting his surgery prepared to make a quick exit as soon as their interview was over. The doctor had perfect timing. Just as they opened the door to re-enter the waiting room, his voice, like a foghorn, gave them a final and embarrassing instruction. Very often it was "Keep your bowels open and fear the Lord!"

Emmie continued to swim and was one of a select group chosen to be coached in diving. This was an honour she could not refuse but she hated it, especially when she had to dive from the top splash, the highest springboard. She could not wait to escape from these lessons and throw her towel down the chute to the laundry. Relieved when these lessons came to an end, Emmie thought she must have been a disappointment to the young man who coached her.

*   *   *   *   *

Autumn not only brought the return to school, it brought harvest time. Farmer Bell watched his ripening corn and kept an eye on the weather. Once the men started cutting the corn, work continued from morning till night. Old and young worked in the fields together. The sheaves of corn had been propped against each other forming tent-like 'stooks'. The children had sometimes played hide-and-seek among them, creeping through the tunnels of prickly stubble. They were always careful not to damage the corn. It was tempting to play, but today the children were expected to help and they set to work with a will.

Emmie and Joe carried the heavy sheaves between them, laughing as the ears of corn dangled in their faces, tickled their noses and made them sneeze. The men passed the sheaves up into the wagons with their long forks. The labourers in the wagon worked quickly, stacking them 'ears in, butts out'. The big shirehorses went to and fro between field and stack yard with their high loads. When the last load of the day was on the wagon, the children climbed up and rode precariously home singing all the way. Next day, threshing would begin.

On wet days, Emmie and her friends frequently played in the barn. It was a good place for hide-and-seek. Sometimes they hid in the loft, peering down through

65

the trap-doors through which the stored hay was dropped. Fortunately, no one ever tumbled through the hole!

In a corner of the barn stood a turnip-slicing machine. Farmer Bell encouraged the children to slice turnips. They took turns to wind the handle round, needing both hands and all their strength. The big wheel gathered momentum, forcing the blades through the turnips. Emmie sniffed energetically as she wound the handle.

"Doesn't it smell lovely?" she sighed ecstatically.

The guardian angels that saved the excited children from falling from the loft must have watched over them as they sliced the turnips. Only turnips were sliced and never fingers. The children turned the handle to the rhythm of an old rhyme. Heaving to start the machine, they chanted slowly,

> *Bread and cheese*
> *Work as you please*
> *Bread and cheese*
> *Work as you please.*

As the wheel turned more easily their chanting grew faster.

> *Bread and cheese and apple pie*
> *Work according-ly!*

With the wheel working at top speed, they panted,

> *Roast beef and plum pudden*
> *Work like a good un!*

They watched as Farmer Bell spread a layer of chaff on the threshing floor and helped him to cover it with a layer of turnip slices. After another layer of chaff and another layer of turnip slices, he poured 'cow treacle' (molasses or black treacle) over the heap. He added hot water and mixed it with a shovel. Then it was ready to feed the cattle. The children's efforts were rewarded by a slice of turnip dipped into the barrel of cow treacle. Emmie's friends regarded this as a treat but Emmie was not keen on eating a cow's dinner. She only liked the smell!

Blackberries were another matter. She loved those. There were always expeditions to pick blackberries in the autumn. The best blackberries grew on each side of Windy House Lane. This was a high spot, dusty in hot weather and muddy in wet weather. The children came home covered in stains and scratches, their mouths purple. Emmie ran in triumphantly with a full basket of fruit. Soon the kitchen was warmed by a good fire – stoked up to heat the oven. The room was fragrant with the delicious aroma of blackberry-and-apple pies baking. After a day in the fresh air, blackberry-and-apple pie, served hot from the oven with custard, was a real treat. Emmie wouldn't have changed places with a millionaire!

*   *   *   *   *

Christmas was not far away when Emmie's teacher, Miss Martin, who was generally kind, examined Emmie's hands. She had noticed that Emmie's fingers were red and chapped and concluded that Emmie had been sucking them.

"I am surprised at you, Emmie!" she scolded, and made her walk round the classroom to demonstrate the consequences of sucking fingers. Emmie was upset but held her tongue. There were only a few days left before the end of term and she made sure her hands were kept out of sight. On the last day of term, Miss Martin asked if Emmie would stay behind to help tidy the classroom. Emmie was pleased to have been chosen for this task but secretly hoped that she would not be too long. Her parents might wonder where she was and regular duties awaited her at the farm. Together they took down paper chains and tidied cupboards. Miss Martin was pleased with their efforts but then realised how dark it was growing. She asked Emmie how far she had to go and was concerned.

Emmie said, "It's alright. I can catch the tram." Around her neck hung two little bags. One contained camphor as a protection against colds and the other a penny for the tram. The tram was only to be used in emergencies. Miss Martin insisted on paying Emmie's fare and accompanying her to explain her lateness. So they rode together and Thomas and Emily were content to learn that their daughter had been useful.

"Would you like a cup of tea and a slice of cake?" asked Emily, and Miss Martin was glad to sit down.

"This fruitcake is delicious!" she said.

Emmie, feeling more relaxed, asked if Miss Martin would like to see the farm. She led her teacher across the road and into the cowshed. Grandad had left the lantern lit for Emmie. At the far end, amid a pile of straw, were two calves. The teacher was enchanted. Emmie fetched a bucket of milk and proceeded to show Miss Martin how she was teaching the calves to drink. Dipping her fingers into the milk she held them out to the calves. Their long tongues wound eagerly round her fingers. This process was repeated over and over again. Emmie was used to their rough tongues lapping every spot of milk.

"Soon, they will be able to drink from a bucket," she told her teacher. Miss Martin realised now why Emmie's fingers were so red.

"I'm so sorry," she said. "I had no idea of what you were doing. I shouldn't have been so hasty. This is my first visit to a farm," she continued. "Watching these calves has been an unforgettable experience. May I come again one day?"

Emmie said that she knew her Grandfather would be glad for Miss Martin to visit whenever she liked. Holding the lantern, Emmie took her to see the horses and the pigs. Then they left the farmyard and waited for the tram.

As Miss Martin climbed on to the tram she called out, "Happy Christmas, Emmie!"

Emmie replied, "Happy Christmas, Miss Martin!" They waved to each other and the tram glided away. Emmie stood transfixed. To think Miss Martin had never been on a farm before! "How lucky I am to live here!" she thought.

Christmas time flew by with the usual family gatherings, and when it was over Emmie's mother began on a big clean. She went through the house from top to bottom. Emily liked to keep her house spick and span. She disliked clutter and thought ornaments collected dust. Emmie had to make sure her books and toys were tidied away or they were relegated to the dustbin. Emily was glad to see the Christmas decorations back in their boxes, and the house was spotless when she noticed a blue balloon that Emmie had been given. It was tied to the end of her bed.

"It makes the place look untidy," she thought and carried it downstairs. "This balloon is in my way," she said and, ignoring Emmie's protests, threw it on the fire.

This time, her impatient action backfired in her face. Instead of catching fire, the balloon was sucked directly up the chimney by the up-draught. Emily tried to reach it with the poker but it rose up the flue and jammed in the pot where it began to expand in the heat. Unable to escape, the smoke was forced back down the chimney and quickly spread throughout the house. While Emily and Emmie struggled and choked below, heat and energy built up in the chimney pot. Suddenly there was an explosion which shattered the pot and removed several bricks from the stack. A great shower of soot, broken pot and strips of balloon descended into the fireplace. There were rumbling noises on the roof and crashing sounds outside as debris descended into the back yard. Neighbours gathered quickly and Thomas came running from his workshop as Emily and Emmie, their eyes red from the smoke, made their way out into the fresh air. Emmie was despatched to fetch the sweep who came immediately. By the time he had finished cleaning the chimney, there was even more soot to be cleared away. Now the kitchen really did need cleaning. Thomas had extra work to do repairing the stack and replacing the pot. Emily admitted that she should have left the balloon tied to the bed!

*   *   *   *   *

January brought snow and the children were very excited. Emmie had a long sledge that Thomas had made and she and Joe trudged up the hill pulling it behind them. Little Jessie plodded along in their tracks hoping for a ride. They went up and over Windy House Lane like Arctic explorers and selected a hill that led down to Prince of Wales Road. Traffic there was sparse and, due to the snow, nothing was moving. This steep slope was very thrilling and the children made several trips. Their scarves blew out behind them. Their cheeks were rosy and glowing. They could all squash on to the sledge. Emmie and Joe took turns at the front.

"It's your go now," said Emmie. Joe settled at the front of the sledge and Emmie sat behind him with Jessie squeezed at the back. She held tight to Emmie's belt.

"Ready?" asked Joe. "Here we go again!" The track had become smoother and faster. Down the hill they swept at glorious speed!

Just as they were reaching the road, a large horse and wagon came round the corner. Stopping was impossible!

Joe shouted, "Lie back!"

All three of them leaned back and prepared for a collision. Emmie closed her eyes and opened them to see the underside of the horse's belly as they shot

between its legs. What a lucky escape! The sledge careered on across the road before coming to a halt in a snowdrift. They crawled out of the snow to see that the horse had stopped and the carter was shaking his head in a bemused way.

Emmie, remembering her manners, approached him nervously and said, "We're very sorry. We must have frightened your horse."

"I don't know as the 'orse is frightened," complained the carter. "But I was scared out of me wits! You kids is lucky to be alive! If you want to stay that way, find somewhere else to do your sledging." He flicked the reins. "Come on, Ned," he called to the horse, and the wagon moved along.

"Thank goodness the sledge is alright," said Joe.

Dark nights and winter evenings brought different pastimes. Sometimes Emmie went with the other children to visit a neighbour, a widow with a sick daughter. The girl could not be left unattended. They each paid a penny to crowd into the tiny room to sit on the bed or on the floor. To earn a little money the lady showed magic lantern slides – coloured pictures, painted on glass, projected on to a white sheet. They seemed magical to Emmie.

Another regular activity was the Saturday night dance at Deep Pits Chapel. Babies and toddlers were bedded down on chairs while their parents tripped the light fantastic or gossiped. Well before it finished, Emmie and Mary Battams walked home together with their families. Emmie and Mary said goodnight at the dairy gate. At the Institute the dancing continued until the late hour of ten o'clock! Of course the Saturday night dance was an opportunity for romance. One day Emmie would find herself perfectly in step with her partner on the dance floor at Deep Pits and forever after. But that was a long way ahead in the future.

February was brightened by Shrove Tuesday. Emily excelled at making pancakes and Emmie excelled at eating them! At this time of year, the Sunday school prizes were awarded. Emmie was always pleased with her prize. Just the feel of a brand new book gave her a thrill. When March arrived, everyone knew that spring was on its way and spirits lifted. Spring brought special joys to the farm. Emmie welcomed hens that had 'laid away' as they ushered their fluffy chicks maternally into the farmyard. The duck pond in the stack yard was full of bobbing ducklings. New life was all around.

There was one never-to-be-forgotten springtime. Emmie's father had bought a little Welsh pony, a wild beast that had not been broken in. The pony was christened Queenie, and Thomas, assisted by Emmie, worked with her regularly. Queenie eventually became a useful horse on the milk round but to begin with she was very nervous. Emmie spent hours gaining Queenie's confidence and was often the only person who could coax her nearer, catch her, and calm her down. Gradually she responded to Emmie's call. Emmie sat on the field wall each day calling gently. At first, Queenie pretended not to hear and circled the field several times. Each time, she came nearer to the wall and finally slowed down by Emmie, tossing her head and pawing the ground. She allowed Emmie to stroke her, and one happy day Emmie managed to slide from the wall on to her back.

What a triumph! Thomas was astonished when he looked across from the dairy to see Emmie riding round the field on Queenie's back. After that Emmie rode Queenie for a short spell each day. Fond dreams of a saddle and a riding outfit never materialised but Emmie became quite skilled as a bareback rider.

As time passed, Thomas realised that Queenie was in foal. "Two for the price of one!" thought Thomas.

Very early, on a spring morning, Emmie was aroused urgently by her mother.

"Emmie! Come and look in the stable!"

Out of bed, downstairs and across the road flew Emmie in her bare feet and nightdress. She ran through the farm gate and into the stable. The newly born foal, struggling to stand, was the most beautiful creature she had ever seen. She knew she would treasure this moment for the rest of her life.

"How clever you are, Queenie!" praised Emmie as the pony nuzzled the tiny foal.

Everyone was delighted with the new arrival. The foal was given the name 'Firefly'. Emmie completely lost her heart to Firefly and anyone searching for Emmie looked in the stable or the field. She spent every spare minute with Queenie and Firefly. The weeks sped by as the little foal grew.

Summer days came and Grandad Evans remembered his promise. He took Emmie and Evelyn, the milk girl, to the seaside. Emmie's mother made each of them a new dress in matching material and their excitement was intense. Grandma Evans was happy to see them going on holiday but  preferred to stay at home. They went on the train, which was a new experience, and stayed in a boarding house. Evelyn, who had not been able to play on a beach before, enjoyed having a bucket and spade like Emmie. Sometimes Grandad sat on the promenade relaxing while the girls made sandcastles or sunbathed in deck chairs. A beach photographer took their picture – a souvenir to take home. Grandad took them on a boat trip, a real adventure. All too soon the holiday was over. Both girls gave him a big hug and thanked him. He was content to know they had enjoyed themselves.

Emmie had other jaunts too. During the summer holidays Emily tried to make time to take Emmie out and usually some of her nephews and nieces too. There was also a substantial picnic packed into the trap. She took Emmie and her cousin Jack to Cordwell Valley. Jack loved riding in the trap and he was allowed to hold the reins for a little while, under his aunt's strict supervision. Emmie was already becoming adept at handling the pony and trap.

On another day, Emily's sister Ada brought Norah and little Teddy to go on a picnic. Teddy was now walking and, as Ada said, 'into everything'. Emmie and Norah were willing nursemaids. Emily drove them to Myrtle Springs where they spread out their picnic a good distance from the cliff top. There was a quarry there with steep sides.

"Goody!" said Norah. "Chocolate cake!"

"Sandwiches first," said Emily. "Egg or potted meat?"

The sandwiches soon disappeared, to be followed by apple pie and cream as well as chocolate cake. There were sighs of satisfaction and they relaxed in the sunshine. Ada's eyes closed and Emily hoped she would have a nap.

"Our Ada looks really tired," she thought. She packed away the picnic and the girls helped.

Suddenly Emmie said, "Where's Teddy?"

She saw him a few yards away, just as he climbed on to the back step of the trap. Topsy, the horse, had been trained to set off when someone put a foot on the step. So, responding to this signal, Topsy moved on. The trap tipped a little and

Teddy was thrown forward into it. Topsy trotted smartly down the slope towards the quarry. Teddy screamed. Emmie raced ahead, managed to catch the reins and shouted, "Whoa!" The horse slowed and stopped, tossing her head wildly. Emmie calmed Topsy while Teddy was being comforted and checked for bumps and bruises. He was shaken, but otherwise unhurt.

Her mother gave Emmie some rare praise. "You were very quick," she said.

Emily had been afraid that the weight of the trap would cause the horse to plunge over the edge. Fortunately, no harm had been done and Emmie was just relieved that Teddy and Topsy were safe.

19. Bringing Home the Cows

Another school year began. Emmie and Joe were soon back into their routine. One morning as they set off for school, Grandad Bell hailed them from across the road.

"Emmie!" he shouted. Both children ran over to him. To Emmie's surprise, he gave her a stout stick. "It's time you learned to bring the cows up for milking," said Grandad. "On your way to school, drop this stick into the cow field and then pick it up after school. You know what to do."

Emmie was nervous but she couldn't refuse Grandad. She took the stick and did as she was told, dropping it into the field.

"Don't worry," said faithful Joe. "I'll help you."

After school the children went into the field.

"Stand by the gate, Joe," instructed Emmie. "Make sure they go up Spring Lane and not down. Bluebell goes first," she added.

Emmie went further into the field and called, "Coo-up! Coo-up!" The cows took no notice. She tried again and they simply carried on chewing the cud and swishing their tails to keep the flies away. "I must try to sound more like Grandad," thought Emmie. She took a deep breath and tried to make her voice as gruff as possible as she shouted loudly, "Coo-up! Coo-up!"

Bluebell raised her head. "Oh, come on, Bluebell!" pleaded Emmie and waved her stick. At last Bluebell began to wander towards the gate. One by one the other cows followed. Emmie rounded up the last one. Joe was manfully blocking the road and Bluebell had made her way up Spring Lane and was just reaching City Road. Emmie ran ahead to make sure that none of the cows fancied a trip into Sheffield. Joe closed the gate and brought up the rear.

At last all the cows were heading up City Road. The children were kept busy, well aware that people would not be pleased to find cows in their front gardens. Of course, most people were used to the cows and didn't mind them. Then a tram came along, and Emmie and Joe tried to move the cows away from the track but without success. Bluebell had no respect for trams or drivers and sauntered along in a very stately fashion. While Emmie tried to redirect Bluebell, Daisy had a sudden impulse to go up a passage! Emmie waved her stick just in time, and the adventurous cow backed out, almost colliding with a horse and cart. The driver shook his head but when he saw a small girl with a big stick emerge from behind the cow, he just grinned. Both children were hot and tired by the time they herded the cows into the stack yard but they were very proud of themselves. Grandad Bell was proud of them too.

"You did a grand job," he told them. "You can do it again tomorrow!"

20. The Storytelling Begins

In 1922, when Emmie was eleven years old, she took a test and was offered a place at the Central School in Sheffield. This was an achievement. It was considered a privilege to go there. Privilege or not, Emmie found this prospect alarming, and was adamant that she preferred to stay with her friends at the Manor Board School. Her parents, knowing that there would be work for her on the milk round, and feeling that her health would benefit from outdoor work, were not anxious about career prospects and let her stay. So Emmie moved into the senior department where the headteacher was Miss Corner, a formidable lady, not quite five feet tall. She ruled with a rod of iron and commanded the respect of the whole school. Emmie liked her because she was fair and didn't have favourites. Miss Corner's hair was taken back into a neat bun. Everything about her was neat and she expected her girls to be the same. Emmie had to kneel in a line with all the other girls while Miss Corner checked that their gym slips were the uniform two inches above the knee.

Emmie didn't like changes but she soon settled in. Changes were taking place all around. A few years before, three terraced houses had been built below the dairy and now more houses were being built along Wulfric Road. The gardens backed on to the side of Emmie's garden. They were the beginning of the Manor Estate, and her grandfather was losing some of his fields. Young families soon were moving in and became good neighbours and customers. The Dickson family lived in the middle terraced house below the dairy. They were good neighbours and Emmie took their daughter Edna to Sunday school. Emmie was upset to hear that they were leaving. Mrs Dickson consoled her.

"Never mind, Emmie. We are not going far and we shall still be coming to Chapel. We are exchanging houses and the people who are coming here have a little girl the same age as Edna."

The Cooper family moved in, and Emmie went to ask if they needed milk or if they had children who would like to go to Sunday school. Mrs Cooper was pleased to have milk delivered and for the children to go to Sunday school. So Emmie called for them each Sunday. She particularly liked little Joyce and was pleased when Joyce joined the Girls Life Brigade. Joyce was not very strong and soon after they moved in she became very ill with chicken pox. A sheet soaked in disinfectant was hung over the door and only her mother went in. Emmie's Grandma Bell went to see her.

"I'm not worried about infection," she said to Mrs Cooper. "If I was going to catch anything, I'd have caught it before now!" Grandma Bell's skills with herbs were well-known and Mrs Cooper was grateful for her help. Joyce recovered but later became ill again with appendicitis. After her appendix was removed, she was in bed for a long time, recovering very slowly. Grandma Bell was once again a daily visitor.

Mrs Cooper declared to Emmie, "Your Grandma has been a wonderful friend to our family."

Grandma Bell had always loved small children so perhaps it was natural for Emmie to love them too. She found she had an easy way with them and often had a procession of younger children following her around. "You are just like the Pied Piper!" said Mrs Cooper. Emmie had always been expected to help with younger cousins and to watch that they did not get into mischief on the farm.

Uncle Walter, who worked on the farm, often had his family there. At that time, he and Aunt Annie had four boys – Walter, Ronnie, Dougie and Kenny. The boys were lively and it was Emmie's regular job to bath them in the copper. The copper was in the outside wash-house. A fire was lit beneath the copper to heat the water. One at a time, they climbed in for Emmie to give them a good scrub.

"Kenny first," said Emmie, helping him to undress. "Walter, be helping Dougie to take his boots off."

The bottom of the copper grew hotter and hotter. Kenny danced about, saying, "Cousin Emmie, my feet are burning!" Emmie lifted him out and put some bricks in for him to stand on, but she was worried that he might trap his toes. She had her work cut out. While one was wrapped in a towel, the next was climbing into the copper.

When all the boys had been hugged dry in their towels, and all the squabbles about vests and socks had been settled, Dougie asked, "Will you tell us a story, Emmie?"

"Tell us about the pig in the sock," said Ronnie.

"No – tell us about Lily Battams in the pig trough," said Walter.

"Well, you must sit quietly," Emmie told them.

The boys scampered across the yard and sat on the hearthrug. Grandma Bell put another log on the fire and it blazed brightly. Emmie passed them all a mug of milk. She pulled up her small stool and sat down.

And so the storytelling began.

21. ENTERTAINMENT

Emmie may have been considered old enough to help but she still enjoyed playing out with the other children. Sometimes their street games were interrupted by the shout of "Motor car!" Such exotic vehicles were still infrequent and caused great excitement. All the children rushed to the edge of the pavement to cheer as the car passed and to wave to the driver. The drivers always waved back. The children were even more excited when Lizzie came into view. Lizzie the elephant had been a familiar sight for a long time at Deep Pits and was a great favourite with the children. The elephant's life had been with the circus until it was 'grounded for the duration' in 1914. Her employers during the war, Messrs. T. Ward, had lost a lot of their horses to war service and Lizzie helped to replace them. Emmie, like all the other children, begged scraps of food to feed to this gentle beast of burden. Lizzie seemed to love the children as much as they loved her.

Working with an elephant did have some disadvantages. Emmie and her parents laughed at a report in the Star, which read '...the elephant had to make a call of nature and made such a mess – and a pong! – that the Fire Brigade had to be called out to clear the mess with their hosepipes. The locals in the area were sent helter-skelter in all directions!' The saying 'You're in a bigger mess than Tommy Ward's elephant!' became commonplace. Lizzie eventually returned to the circus but died in 1922. All Sheffield mourned her passing.

Emmie was now even more involved in church and brigade activities. She and Lily Hanson were always eager to take part in all the concerts and festivities. Their help with the younger children was welcomed. Her mother, who was handy with a needle, made all kinds of costumes for their performances. Sometimes Emily helped Mrs Battams with costumes for Mary and Lily. The children rehearsed for months, and their parents were told in good time what they would need to wear, but somehow Mrs Battams was never ready. The big concert of the year was given on New Year's Day. Mrs Battams was only just recovering from Christmas and the atmosphere was strained as she tried to gather the costumes together.

Each year Mary's mother vowed, "This concert will be the last!" and roped all the neighbours in to help her at the last minute. When the concert was a great success and Mary and Lily excelled themselves, Mr and Mrs Battams glowed with pride and the stress of costume-making was forgotten.

Poor Mrs Battams was not only expected to sew for concerts. All the ladies were expected to stitch, crochet or knit for the bazaar. All kinds of craft were welcomed and baking was almost compulsory! The bazaar lasted for three days. Work for this went on all year round. Where did all the aprons, doilies and needle cases go?

At the spring fair there were additional stalls representing different sections of the Church, and sometimes these stalls stocked specialist goods like cutlery. Emmie helped to hang garlands of lemon and green crepe paper flowers. She thought the spring fair was very pretty. This fair lasted for several days and so overnight watches were mounted. Thomas sometimes watched for a few hours but this was mainly a task for the younger men.

If Emmie thought that the spring fair was pretty she could not find words to describe the Harvest Festival. Harvest was truly a time for rejoicing. Tables were covered in snowy cloths, and heavily laden with produce. Those who kept allotments brought their best vegetables and their largest marrows. Emmie helped her father to cut armfuls of flowers from the garden. Housewives contributed sparkling jars of bottled plums and jam. All available surfaces were bright with flowers. Everything was arranged with meticulous care and the simple church was truly beautiful. Farmer Bell sent a large sheaf of corn as a centrepiece. Emmie shared in the joy he felt to see it spread at the base of the table among baskets of apples and potatoes.

"Doesn't the corn look lovely, Grandad?" she said.

"It does that!" replied Grandad.

A golden loaf was baked in the shape of a sheaf of corn. The children searched for the tiny mouse, which was always somewhere, climbing a corn stalk. At the centre of the harvest table were the basic necessities of life – a polished piece of coal, a gleaming glass of water, and a saltcellar. When all was ready, old and young gazed upon their work with satisfaction. A memorable fragrance of flowers, earthy vegetables, dusty cornstalks and ripe fruit filled the air.

At the Harvest service Emmie stood between her grandparents and quietly made sure their hymn books were the right way up. Neither of them could read. It didn't make any difference. They knew the words by heart. Their favourite hymn was 'Come Ye Thankful People, Come'. Emmie and all her farming family were only too glad to give thanks for a harvest safely gathered. Very often the choir gave a well-practised rendition of 'Ruth'. Emmie grew to know all the different singing parts and sometimes the dairy echoed with the family version. In church she occasionally suppressed a smile. She liked to hear the men when they pressed their chins against their chests and growled, "…and dip thy morsel in the vin-e-gar!"

Following Harvest Sunday came the Monday 'pea and pie supper'. All the ladies carried their homemade pies and handed them over to those in charge. In theory it was 'pot-luck' as to whose pie was served to any table, but human nature is such that certain pies were noted. Emmie's mother was renowned for her baking and her pie was usually kept back for one of the servers. Emmie never forgot the supper when her mother broke open the crust of the pie delivered to their table and found whole, large potatoes, still hard, inside. They all laughed. "Well, everybody has to learn," said Emily.

Once supper was cleared away, everyone waited with anticipation for the auction of the produce. Emmie was proud of her Grandad who took his place at the front supported by his friend, John Oxley. Farmer Bell, in his old brown smock, knew how to entertain his audience. Auctions at cattle markets were a part of his life and his patter moved the sale along quickly. He did not have the local accent and the way he spoke attracted attention. There was plenty of answering back from the audience.

"What am I bid for these very fine tatties?" he said. "They look as if they're out of Bell's fields," he added, and immediately had a response.

"Nay Walter, them tatties are a sight better'n yourn. Yourn are tiddlers compared with them!"

Much laughter followed this exchange and the bidding began.

"Now then, gentlemen," called Walter. "How about a lovely bouquet of flowers or a basket of fruit to give to your beautiful wives? Come on ladies, give your husbands a nudge!"

A sheepish-looking fellow blurted out, "Twopence, Farmer Bell."

"Threepence!" shouted another.

So it went on till the first fellow blushingly collected his flowers and handed them to his wife amid cheers and ribald comments. Walter knew his audience and played to them. Meanwhile, Emmie and her friends were kept busy delivering fruit and vegetables to their purchasers. Most people had brought roomy bags made of oilcloth to carry home their bargains. They expected bargains and no fancy prices were paid. They had already given of their best and money was not easy to come by. Helpers like Emmie were often given an apple or a pear as a reward for their labours. Little Joyce Cooper, scuttling under a table to retrieve a lost fruit, discovered it was not an orange but something more exotic. It was the first pomegranate she had ever seen. She carried it to Farmer Bell who looked down at her with a smile.

"It's called a pomegranate," he told her. "You can keep it."

"Farmer Bell gave me a pomegranate!" Joyce said to Emmie, her eyes wide in wonder.

Finally, every cabbage and carrot was sold and there was a round of applause. The tables were cleared away, the floor was swept, and the pie dishes returned to their owners. Everyone went home laden with good things but little Joyce carried home the greatest treasure of all, her precious pomegranate.

22. The Man in the Suit

Soon after Emmie's move into the secondary department, her Grandma, Harriet Evans, died. Emmie was very sorrowful, not just for herself, but for her Grandad. He came to see them and said to Emmie, "I've brought you something to remember your Grandma by." He lifted a parcel out of his bag for Emmie to open. There lay the little cherry-red shawl that Grandma had always worn. Emmie thought it was pretty. She tied it round her neck with the little woollen tassels and Grandad watched her with a tear in his eye. "I shall keep it for ever," Emmie told him. "Thank you, Grandad."

Grandma's death brought a big change to Emmie's life, but changes were taking place all around. Unemployment was spreading and poverty was increasing. Those

who had survived the battles of the war had come home, not to a hero's welcome but very often to find that their jobs were no longer there for them. Mr Dickson, their former neighbour and a skilled tailor in his father's family firm, had been rejected by his own father and, along with many others, had to search for work. Fortunately he obtained a post as commissionaire at the large General Post Office in Sheffield. With his military bearing, he looked very smart in his uniform, his empty sleeve folded neatly into his pocket. He became a familiar, trusted figure with a smile for everyone. No one was left feeling lost in that vast building. He made sure of that. On numerous occasions he took people home for the night when he found they had missed their train. The station was close by and people in difficulties often sought help at the Post Office. Mr Dickson was grateful for his work. Many men could not find jobs and those who did strove to keep them.

So Emmie was shocked when her wily Aunty Florrie feigned illness to avoid work. Florrie had always been the odd one out in the family. She was very eccentric and occasionally an embarrassment to them. Emmie loved her and was pleased to find her at home in the farmhouse one day when she expected her to be at work. Emmie thought she must be on holiday and greeted her with a hug. Aunty Florrie rummaged in her voluminous apron pocket and pulled out a paper bag of boiled sweets.

"Sithee, Emmie," she said. "Have a spice."

Grandma Bell was out visiting a sick neighbour and Aunty Florrie was cleaning up. Emmie helped her to shake the rugs outside in the yard and went with her to make the beds. Back in the kitchen she helped her aunt to dry the dishes. Emmie thought her aunt was acting strangely and wondered why she kept peering through the window. Suddenly Aunty Florrie said, "Sithee, Emmie, run and look if a man in a suit is getting off the tram. If he walks up the road, come quick and tell me."

Emmie jumped down the farmhouse steps and peered round the gatepost. No suit-clad man emerged from the tram, which sailed back down City Road.

"There isn't a man, Aunty," called Emmie. Aunt Florrie looked relieved. She continued to peer through the window and kept an eye on the clock. Every time a tram was due, Emmie was sent to look for a man in a suit. After several trams, a man in a suit descended from a tram and Emmie rushed back shouting, "He's coming, Aunty!"

Florrie picked up an enormous shawl and threw it over her head. She fell into the rocking-chair and, to Emmie's astonishment, began to groan dramatically, rocking back and forth, wailing and crying loudly. A knock came at the door and

Emmie invited the man in nervously. He observed this scene apprehensively and then asked, "Excuse me, madam, are you Florice Bell?"

Aunt Florrie continued to groan and the man looked at Emmie.

Emmie swallowed nervously and nodded.

The man looked dismayed and very soon retreated, murmuring apologies for having disturbed her when she was so ill. He was soon whisked away on the next tram. Aunt Florrie kept up her pretence until Emmie reassured her that he had really departed. Then, miraculously, the moaning stopped. The shawl was folded and Aunt Florrie beamed at Emmie.

"Thank goodness he's gone!" she exclaimed.

When Emmie went home she described Florrie's antics to her parents. They looked at each other and chuckled.

"That's our Florrie!" said Emily. "We'll never change her."

"She was afraid she'd lose her job," said Thomas. "But don't go thinking that's the right thing to do." Emmie looked indignant and Thomas smiled. "No," he said. "You would never do that. You are too honest."

To be fair to Aunt Florrie, she did have long periods of working reliably. Tuckwoods, a well-established restaurant, employed her for washing-up duties. Never one for missing an opportunity, Aunty Florrie realised that waste food was being thrown away daily. Having gained permission, she took two buckets to work every day. Any leftovers or stale food were tipped into them and she brought them home on the tram for pigswill. No one chose to sit next to her! Most of the passengers turned up their noses. Aunty Florrie was happily oblivious of her isolation and the pigs, on their high-class diet, were most appreciative!

23. The Thrift Class

In 1924, the people of Sheffield experienced a terrifying tropical storm. The night was incredibly hot and Emmie tried to ignore the first rumblings of thunder and flashes of lightning. She was relieved when the bedroom door was pushed open and Jack came to keep her company. The old dog was as frightened as she was. He hid under the bed and Emmie, with her pillow on the bedside mat, stayed close to him. It was a long night and Emmie hated the thunder and lightning. When a brief lull in the storm brought some relief, she went to the window to look out.

"The sky is green!" she told Jack.

Finally, the rain descended in torrents and by morning the worst of the storm was over. Emmie, after an almost sleepless night, rose early with her parents. After her breakfast she ran to let the hens out as usual. The garden was drenched, plants were flattened and branches had fallen from the apple tree. Emmie reached the hen house, lifted the flap and called out, "Come on, hens. Chuck! Chuck! Chuck!" She waited for the usual clamour of clucking, bright-eyed hens pushing and jostling their way out but all was quiet.

"Surely they are not still asleep," thought Emmie and opened the door to peer in. "Yes they are!" she said. "They are still on their perch." She shook her bucket of corn and threw down a handful, calling, "Wake up! Chuck! Chuck!" There was no response and a shiver ran down Emmie's spine. She stepped through the gloom of the hen-house and reached out to touch one of the hens. It didn't move and, in that instant, Emmie realised they were all dead. She dropped the bucket and flew down the garden to tell her parents. They thought the bad night must have affected her nerves. They followed her back up the garden and peered through the door. Perhaps the hens were frozen with fear? No, they were all dead. They did not appear to be injured and it was eerie and upsetting.

'The Great Storm of 1924' had been the worst on record and many strange stories were told about it. Emmie was shaken by this experience but as the days passed she found many other things to occupy her mind. Her busy life was a constant round of helping in the dairy and on the farm, attending church and brigade activities. Soon, she knew, there would be changes at school.

*   *   *   *   *

In September, Emmie entered her last year at school and moved into the 'Thrift Class'. This class prepared the girls to run a home economically and efficiently. There were twenty-four girls in the class. Numbers were limited because the room only provided for twenty-four. Two of the Manor girls had to go to Intake. Each girl in the thrift class needed two aprons – a working apron and a cookery apron. The girls made their own aprons under Miss Corner's keen supervision. Emmie found this a long and laborious task. The aprons had very long strings, which were hand-stitched. Every six stitches she had to show her work to Miss Corner. If the stitches were not small and identical they had to be taken out.

At last the aprons were finished but there was more sewing. The girls had to learn to 'make do and mend', how to turn worn sheets 'sides to middle', and how to darn. They made kettle holders and iron holders to lift these burning hot implements. The holders consisted of two crocheted or knitted squares enclosing several layers of flannel. Emmie had already learned some of these skills from her mother.

Laundry was important too. Garments were expensive to buy or to make and had to last. Miss Meek, teacher in the thrift class, asked the girls to bring their best Sunday knickers to school labelled with their own names. Realising that the girls from the Children's Home would be unlikely to possess such garments, she asked if any girls could bring two pairs. Emmie was able to take two pairs but she felt unhappy about the girls from the home. There were two local homes – a home for boys above the cemetery and a home for girls below the cemetery. Emmie wondered if the girls from the home felt embarrassed at not being able to bring their own knickers.

The girls learned to light a fire and heat the water in the copper. By the time the Sunday knickers had been boiled and rinsed they were whiter than white. All the girls would be using these skills after schooldays were over. Some would be dependent on them to earn a living. Women often took in washing and it was not unusual for 'better-off' families to employ them.

Emmie and her mother were amused to read a note pinned to a friend's laundry. Accidentally, a rag that had been used as a duster covered in Brasso had been included. The note read: 'Washed and ironed – one knicker leg – couldn't find the other'. Laundry involved other skills such as starching and ironing. Emmie and her classmates had to master handling heavy flatirons. They had to recognise when an iron became cool and select another. Emmie's seat was near to the stove where all the irons were heated and she was often hot and uncomfortable.

The day came when the teacher began to show them the way to use an iron. How would they know if an iron were hot enough to use? The teacher demonstrated. Holding the iron in her right hand with the flat surface of the iron towards the class, she wet the fingertips of her left hand with the tip of her tongue. A lightning-fast dab with her wet fingers on the surface of the iron produced an audible sizzle. The teacher explained to her attentive class that the sizzle proved that the iron was ready for use. Emmie guessed what was coming next and, along with all the other girls, selected a hot iron. They were instructed to line up in a military fashion and then turn so that they were all in a straight queue in front of the teacher. Every girl held her iron in her right hand

with the flat surface of the iron facing forward. One by one they had to demonstrate to the teacher the testing of the iron. That was the plan but the girl at the front was understandably nervous. Hesitantly, she prepared to touch the hot iron but lost confidence at the last moment and jerked her elbow backwards, letting out a scream as her elbow touched the hot iron of the girl behind. A chain reaction of arm-jerking and elbow-burning flew down the line with squeals of pain, gasps of shock, and accusations. Somehow the teacher restored order and the hot irons were replaced on the stove. Emmie went home with a sore elbow but her parents, while sympathetic, never thought of complaining. No one did. Life was tough anyway and what was a little skin off an elbow?

24. The Milk Round

"Emmie Evans! Miss Corner wants to see you immediately."

Emmie looked up from her sewing with wide eyes. "Yes, Miss Meek," she responded politely. As she hastily removed her cap and apron her thoughts raced, searching for anything she could have done to warrant a summons from her head teacher. The other girls stared as she left the room.

Emmie knocked on the door marked 'Head Teacher' and heard Miss Corner's clear voice call, "Come in."

To Emmie's relief she was greeted with a smile and actually invited to sit down. She perched on the edge of a chair, still in some apprehension.

"I have been informed by Sheffield City Council that they have a vacancy for a messenger," said Miss Corner. "They have asked me if there is a reliable and intelligent school leaver who would be interested in the post. The job would involve delivering messages between departments and various buildings. Sometimes letters would have to be taken into schools. You will be fourteen soon and leaving us. I should like to put your name forward if your parents agree. Please discuss it with them." She added, "A uniform would be provided."

"Thank you, Miss Corner," said Emmie and returned to her class, her mind racing faster than ever.

At home she and her parents considered this new idea.

"How kind of Miss Corner to choose you!" her mother exclaimed. Her father looked thoughtfully at Emmie.

"It's a good opportunity," he remarked. "How do you feel about it, Emmie?"

Emmie hesitated. "I'm pleased Miss Corner asked me and I do not like to say no, but I would rather help you with the milk round."

Her parents gave relieved smiles, and assured her that she was wanted and needed on the milk round and in the dairy, but they would have supported her choice to work as a messenger. "Miss Corner will understand," they said. Miss Corner did understand and wished Emmie well.

So, when Emmie was fourteen, she left the Manor Board School and began work immediately. She was already familiar with work in the dairy and on deliveries but, even so, she felt a flicker of excitement on her first official day. She was up very early to help to harness the horse. Working with the horses was the main attraction of the milk round for Emmie. She helped her father to strap the two fifteen-gallon churns on to the milk float and hung the ladles round them. These ladles, with long, curved handles, filled the cans in which milk was carried to the houses. Smaller measures were used to fill the jugs and basins left on windowsills and doorsteps. Emmie had a brand new, specially made can, smaller than the rest. Thomas always made sure that younger helpers were not overloaded. Emmie's cousins, Jack and Leonard, helped at the weekends and each had their own can.

Emmie was very quick arithmetically and part of her work was collecting payment. There were a few initial problems since a few customers were crafty and recognised her naivety. They did their best to distract her, keep her waiting, and then swear they had paid. One particular family was skilled at these tactics.

"Show Emmie your new comic," they would say, knowing that Emmie always spoke to the children. On one memorable occasion, they pulled her in to show her their new game. They wound up the shabby gramophone and seated the baby (minus nappy) on the turntable! The baby, beaming and gurgling, revolved slowly. Afterwards Emmie confessed that she was sure she had not been paid. Her father gave her strict instructions to concentrate. Emmie soon became used to their wily ways and learned how to deal with them.

Deep Pits Dairy had an extensive milk round so there was plenty of walking. Thomas, Evelyn and Emmie had short rides on the float now and again, but there was not much room and the horse already had enough weight to pull. Emmie's mother was most often at the reins. People frequently ran out with jugs and she would ladle their milk straight from the churn. As the level of the milk in the churns dropped, their positions in the float needed adjusting to balance the float. Emily had to move carefully to serve from the churns.

92

Emmie was always glad to reach Bernard Street in the Park District where her Grandad Evans lived and worked. She took his milk every day and gave him a hug and a kiss. She knew he was pleased to see her.

Emmie was very happy in her work but had trouble in severe winter weather because she was prone to chilblains. Her customers were sympathetic and the Richardson family at number 636 City Road was particularly kind. Mr Richardson had a soft spot for the little milk girl. He had known her since she was born.

"Come in, Emmie," he insisted. "Sit down for a moment. Alice, bring a bowl of warm water." He quickly removed her boots and socks, and her swollen and inflamed feet were immersed in lukewarm water. Mrs Richardson dried her feet quickly and tenderly, and Emmie had a little relief from the awful irritation.

Emmie never forgot their kindness. Little did she know then that, one day, they would be her mother and father-in-law. Mr Richardson always pinned his first Christmas rose to her overall. Christmas roses from his plants would always thrive in her gardens. Emmie was thrilled with her first buttonhole.

*　　*　　*　　*　　*

One day, Emmie was busy in the dairy when, through the open door, she saw her father leading a new horse into the stack yard. Eager to see, she rushed across. Immediately, she loved the new horse and he responded to her, pushing his nose into her shoulder.

"What is his name?" she asked.

"Jimmy," said Thomas. "They tell me he was in the war." He spoke to Jimmy. "You won't be a warhorse here, Jimmy." Then he asked, "Where's your mother?"

Emmie replied, "She's ratting for Grandad. She's taken the dog and Grandad's gun and—" She had not finished speaking when there was a loud shot! The new horse gave a start. Emmie thought that he was going to rear up, but he froze to the spot and stood rigidly. Only his eyes rolled, showing his fear. While they were reassuring him, Emily came round the corner of the barn and saw them. She was sorry to hear that the gunshot had frightened Jimmy on his first day and promised him she would never shoot again while he was close by.

Jimmy adapted easily and became a very reliable horse, pulling the milk float steadily. It was one wintry afternoon, as they were trotting along Stafford Road, that he gave them a big surprise. Emily was driving and Emmie was with her in the float. Ahead of them the Salvation Army had arranged themselves into a circle in the spacious entrance to Norfolk Park. A dramatic drum-roll led into an energetic rendering of 'We Are Marching to Zion'. Jimmy halted as the drums began. Suddenly he was a changed horse. He seemed to grow and his head lifted proudly. His ears stood to attention. Then, with great deliberation, he began to march to the music!

Emily and Emmie looked at each other in astonishment. Thomas, waiting for them on the corner, stared in amazement at this high-stepping horse progressing regally toward him. Jimmy was on parade!

They swung into the turning circle of the park entrance and the Salvation Army stopped playing to admire him. Emmie was so proud of him!

"We'll play you on your way," said the Captain and the band struck up with 'Onward Christian Soldiers'.

A few months later, out on the daily round, Emmie returned to the float after taking milk to a customer and found her father talking to a stranger. The man had recognised Jimmy as the horse he had ridden in the war. It had obviously been a close partnership and Emmie was not surprised to see tears in his eyes.

"Jimmy was so brave," he told them. "Even when he was terrified in the middle of fighting, he never threw me. We survived together. I am so glad to know that he has a good home." It was a joyful reunion.

Now that Emmie knew his history, she loved Jimmy even more. At that time bands were very popular. Every outdoor social event involved a band so Jimmy was able to demonstrate his talents on many occasions. A roll of drums, a fanfare of trumpets, and Jimmy was once more a warhorse!

*   *   *   *   *

Thomas found that he had problems when the Co-op tried to establish milk deliveries, forcing some small dairies out of business. The Co-op also began to sell pasteurised milk, causing some of his customers to have doubts. Thomas was proud of his milk and complained, "Sterilized, past-your-eyes, and mesmerized! They are taking all the goodness out of the milk." He had blotters made advertising his 'Pure, unadulterated milk'. He and other dairymen met together to discuss their problems.

While a friendly rivalry existed between them, the dairymen tended to help each other. Two good friends were Jim and Carrie Flint. They had a farm and a milk round near Norfolk Park. Jim and Carrie Flint, with their weather-beaten and smiling faces, were always pleased to see Emmie. The ancient farmhouse fascinated Emmie. Legend had it that Mary Queen of Scots had escaped from Manor Castle and sought refuge in the farmhouse. She had declared the farmhouse to be 'an arbour in the thorne'. Emmie wondered if the farmhouse was haunted.

95

"Well" – Carrie paused – "there is a room we never use. There's an eerie feeling about it. We never go in there."

Emmie went home to dream wildly about Mary Queen of Scots wandering through Flint's farm. Was there any truth in the story? Who knows? Some years later an estate would be built nearby called Arbourthorne.

Jim Flint, Thomas, and the other dairymen stood their ground together and the Co-op was, at that time, unsuccessful in taking their trade.

Some people may have considered that Thomas was old-fashioned in his contempt for pasteurised milk, but in many ways he was forward-thinking. Emmie was very impressed when he brought a shining new churn into the dairy.

"This is the first seamless churn in Sheffield!" he announced. "It is the latest thing in modern hygiene." Poor Thomas! A few weeks later, a visiting inspector pronounced it unuseable because of incorrect capacity. To make certain it would not be used again, the inspector hit it with a hammer kept for the purpose of rendering inaccurate containers completely unfit. The churn was well and truly dented. Fortunately for Thomas, the churn had been correctly manufactured and he was able to prove the inspector wrong. Thomas was vindicated and the churn was replaced. The whole family rejoiced.

The daily milk round continued and Emmie, with her parents, was up with the lark, winter and summer. There was another member of their team: Emmie's Old English sheepdog, Jack, considered himself one of the staff. He assumed he was in charge and supervised everybody, making sure they all returned to their posts. Jack kept a special eye on Emmie, following her up and down passages and waiting outside shops. He paused occasionally for children to fuss him. However, when Thomas called him there was instant obedience.

Emmie grew to know her customers well. Everyone had a word for her and some of her customers smiled to see her dancing up City Road on her homeward journey. Returning with empty churns, Emmie made the milk float even lighter by walking beside the horse and leading him with the reins. Convinced that if Jimmy could march to the music he should surely be able to waltz, she sang to him "One, two, three – one, two, three!" over and over again. Sadly, Jimmy never mastered ballroom dancing.

Emmie's happy nature helped her to see the best in the most difficult of customers. She always remembered to stop whistling at the Shrewsbury Almshouses because it upset the old man who lived in the end house.

He told her, "A whistling woman and a crowing hen bring the old lad out of his den."

He was genuinely afraid that the Devil would appear and whisk her away!

Another cantankerous customer regularly complained that her milk was not fresh. She was convinced that fresh milk should still be warm. Fortunately, she lived near to the farm and Emmie made an effort to please her, often taking her milk straight from the cow.

When new customers moved into the area, it was Emmie's task to visit them. She gave them a blotter with details of the dairy and asked politely if they would like their milk delivering. She also asked if they had children who would like to go to Sunday school and offered to collect them. Very often they responded positively and everyone benefited. Emmie found her work full of interest.

Thomas looked at her one night as they sat round the fire after the long day's work.

"Do you ever wish you had taken that job as a messenger?" he asked.

"Never!" Emmie answered. She watched the flames lighting up the old Yorkshire range and felt absolute contentment. "Never!" she repeated. "Working on the milk round is where I belong."

25. A Struggle to Survive

Emmie was always grateful for the skills learned in the thrift class, but she had been brought up with the philosophy of 'waste not, want not'. She considered herself fortunate to have work in 1926 when the General Strike increased poverty and hardship. For many people it was a struggle to survive. There was no Social Security safety net and the Workhouse was dreaded. Medical treatment was costly. Extended families and good neighbours looked after each other. Thomas, with his shoemaking skills and the milk round, tried to support other family members and neighbours. Emily's brother, Billy, had a big family and Thomas employed his son, Leonard, on the milk round. Leonard's brother, Jack, worked with him at the weekends. Emily always made sure that her nephews had a good meal at the end of the day.

Thomas's shoemaking and mending enabled him to pay others for small duties. At that time he had no stitching facilities. The shoes had to be taken into Sheffield for stitching and there was always someone glad to take on this errand. Stitching cost sixpence a pair. Every day, friends and unemployed neighbours gathered in Thomas's workshop. Thomas enjoyed company and was never distracted from his work. The men sat on a long bench enjoying the warmth from the pot-bellied stove. Beyond the stove Thomas worked at his bench under the window. On the end wall were shelves and above them were pigeonholes with a wide range of contents: nails of all shapes and sizes; round studs for workmen's boots; cards of 'segs'; heel and toe irons, roughly cut; over-sized leather soles; thick rubber soles cut from sheet rubber; and 'bought-in' soles for nailing on to the shoes.

There were various machines – buffing wheels, grinding wheels, and emery wheels. The emery wheel ground the leather to an exact fit. On the bench, a paraffin burner kept tools hot in the flame. Thomas dipped these in coloured wax – there were sticks of different colours – and ran the wax round the seals. Then he polished them on the buffing wheel so that the edges of the heels and toes shone. Under the bench was a large bucket of diluted ammonia to soak and soften the leather. Emmie liked to watch her father, and sometimes he allowed her to help with small tasks. When the men began to gather, usually in the afternoon, he would say, "Run along and help your mother." Most of the men smoked and the smoke, mixed with the smell of ammonia, produced a pungent atmosphere that could not be described as healthy.

Other people were trying to make life easier for the unemployed. Soup kitchens were set up in some places and one was provided at the Traveller's Rest. This was quite a smart establishment. Arthur Mirfin, the landlord, believed in keeping up standards. He wouldn't serve any woman unless she was wearing a hat! The Traveller's Rest had a garden and a well-kept bowling green. Emmie's friend, Mary Battams, heard shouting and laughter from the garden as she was coming home from school, and peered through the hedge. Through the leaves she saw a crowd of children who appeared to be having a party. Quite indignant that she, who lived in Deep Pits, had not been invited, she ran home to complain to her mother.

"Why can't I go to the party?" she demanded. Her mother explained, and told her firmly that she was fortunate to come home to a proper dinner. Despite being well-fed, Mary continued to feel deprived at not being allowed to eat the bread and dripping provided at the Traveller's Rest. Emmie, old enough to understand, was haunted by the suffering she saw in the faces of the miners.

Behind the Traveller's Rest was a large area where the remains of the deep pits, which gave the village its name, could still be seen. An old shaft, commonly called a ginn pit stood there. It was surrounded by a high wall and the children threw stones over the wall. They were convinced that the resulting echoes came from ghosts!

The mines were probably worked from the seventeen hundreds to the late eighteen hundreds. They were worked out before the nearest mines, Handsworth Nunnery and Woodburn Nunnery, were opened. During the working of Deep Pits, the miners would have forked through the coal to separate the large pieces of coal for the 'large coal' market. The 'slack' (the small coal) fell through the tines of the forks and was wheelbarrowed away or pushed in small tubs to the spoil heaps. These mounds were never higher than twenty-five feet. In 1926, the area consisted of large humps and hollows with the dross still visible in places. During the strike, and at any other time of hardship, whole families worked there. Some of them came from other villages and walked a long way. At Deep Pits there was no charge for collecting slack, but at some of the old mines, like Birley, a ticket had to be purchased. Scavenging for coal was hard and dirty work but even a small fire, burning fitfully, was better than nothing. All kinds of containers were filled and carried home gladly. After this hard work it is unlikely that they had the luxury of tin baths filled with warm water. Water, heated over such precious fires, was used for more important purposes like cooking.

Emmie was thankful that she never had to dig for coal. She worked hard on the milk round and was grateful that her father had two strings to his bow. Many people were superstitious and there was a general belief that 'shoes on the table bring bad luck'. Emmie, robustly against the foolishness of superstition, declared, "Shoes on the table bring good luck because they bring work!"

26. LUCKY

One of Emmie's daily tasks was to set out saucers of milk for the semi-wild cats that roamed around the farm. Milk was plentiful and the cats earned it by keeping down the rats and mice. Finding a pathetic black and white kitten one frosty morning, Farmer Bell took pity on it. He carried it into the farmhouse and in the warmth of the kitchen, the kitten revived. Ellen took a fancy to the little ball of fur and her grandchildren loved it. The kitten was lucky enough to become the house cat and a family pet. Lucky never seemed to forget that Walter had been his rescuer and became very attached to him. Wherever Walter went, the cat was never far away. If Walter was milking the cows, Lucky would be in the cowshed. He followed Walter into the fields and sometimes rode on the farm cart. He was a companionable cat and Walter was very fond of him.

Towards the end of summer, Walter was trying out some haymaking cutting machinery. The horse was plodding along steadily and the machine rattled behind. At the end of the field they swung round and, as the cutter moved into the longer hay, Walter was horrified to see Lucky in its path. Walter stopped his horse almost on the instant but it was too late. Lucky shot out of the machine and streaked across the field. Walter saw with dismay that Lucky had lost a hind leg. He found the tangled limb among the machinery. Walter's heart was heavy as he returned to the farm. Hopefully Lucky would have sought comfort there. But Ellen had not seen him and they were both distraught. Emmie was sent to tell friends and neighbours and there was a wide search for the injured cat. He was not found. Days passed and then weeks. Walter was sure Lucky had crawled under a hedge to die.

Three months later Walter came in from the fields and sat down in his chair. The house was quiet.

"Ellen must be over the road," thought Walter. He closed his eyes and savoured the peace and quiet. A few moments later he was asleep. He must have dozed for half an hour when voices outside broke into his sleep. Eyes still shut, he heard the door open. As Ellen and Emmie came in, he woke fully.

"Well! Dang my eyes!" he exclaimed as they came round his chair. They all stared in astonishment. There was Lucky asleep on Walter's lap! Lucky seemed quite unconcerned about the fuss that was made. It was just as if he had never been away. Emmie was amazed at how well he managed with only three legs.

"It was a good name for him after all," she said. "He's lucky to be alive."

*　　*　　*　　*　　*

"Dang my eyes!" was the nearest Walter Bell ever came to swearing. Secretly, it amused Emmie but she never smiled because she knew her grandmother did not approve of bad language. This did not prevent Walter from expressing his feelings with this well-used phrase.

Emmie's younger cousin, Joy, who lived at Doncaster, had been seriously ill with diphtheria. When she left the isolation department of Conisbrough Hospital, her parents decided she would benefit from a stay at the farm. Joy, still weak and listless, did not settle. Grandma Bell was very anxious. She went across to the dairy and told Emily, "The child is hardly eating anything and she doesn't want to play. I'm really worried." Emily thought that perhaps Emmie could help.

"I'll send her across with some jelly," she said.

So Emmie went to play with Joy and they looked at books together. But in spite of Emmie's best efforts, Joy was still withdrawn and unhappy.

It was soon realised that Joy needed more medical attention and she was taken to hospital in Sheffield for a tonsillectomy. Her adenoids were removed as well. When Grandma Bell brought her home, Emmie was helping Grandad in the farm kitchen. Joy was as white as a ghost and still sickly from the ether. She started to climb the stairs and halfway up turned giddy and fell to the bottom. Grandad quickly picked her up and examined her. She was bumped and bruised but no bones were broken. Grandma Bell took her on her knee in the big rocking-chair to comfort her. Grandad, shocked and feeling responsible, exclaimed, "Dang my eyes, Ellen! This child will be the death of me!"

Grandma stopped rocking and looked at him severely.

"Mr Bell!" she said. "Not in front of the children!" Arrested by this adult interchange, Joy forgot herself and gave Emmie a tiny smile and a knowing look. Emmie smiled back and, at that moment, a bond was established between them. They would always be friends.

27. Everybody Sing!

The audience clapped enthusiastically as, two by two, the children took their bow in the finale of 'Little Red Riding Hood'. Lily Hanson and Emmie made their curtsey together, and the stage was full of excited youngsters. The audience consisted of proud parents and grandparents. This homespun and light-hearted entertainment was typical of Deep Pits Sunday school. All the children were encouraged to join in, and considered to have some talents to contribute. As time went by, Emmie, Lily and their friends graduated from these simple shows to more ambitious productions. Deep Pits Institute staged some highly successful performances. Sheffield people enjoyed amateur and professional theatre and music. Local shows were an important part of general culture. A spirit of competition and rivalry abounded as people travelled to watch each other's productions.

Deep Pits was fortunate in having Ron Wolfenden and his talented wife, Edna, to lead them. Working together, with Ron producing and Edna at the piano, they were a good team. They attended all the productions of the Sheffield Operatic Society and each time came home inspired. Edna always sat down at the piano and played the music all the way through from memory, while they both sang long into the night. They expected and received high standards from the cast. Emmie and Lily, progressing to these serious productions, had to make a proper commitment. They both joined the church choir and found their lives full of rehearsals and practices.

During the Christmas season, the choir generally gave a performance of 'The Messiah'. This was a highlight of the Christian year. Mr Buckland rehearsed his choir long and hard for this event. They had a reputation to keep. People came from surrounding areas to listen, and a small orchestra was hired. On one occasion, the invited pianist failed to appear. A universal sense of pride was felt when their own Edna Wolfenden took her place at the piano and played perfectly.

The first time Emmie sang in 'The Messiah', she was conscious of being part of a wonderful tradition. She had heard it many times before and knew that all around the world voices were being raised in this magnificent music. She was part of that voice! She concentrated hard as the great crescendo grew. Then there was the heart-stopping, famously dramatic silence. Deep Pits may have been a simple wooden church, but the power of 'The Messiah' was as strong as if it had been St Paul's Cathedral.

* * * * *

The Girls Life Brigade still played a big part in Emmie's busy life. She had joined when the company was formed and had revelled in all the activities. She had worked for badges and played games. There had been frequent 'nature walks' and she had made a book of pressed flowers. The brigade had widened her horizons and brought her many friends. When she was seventeen she attended a meeting with all the leaders and senior girls. Emmie was surprised and delighted to be asked if she would take charge of the cadets, the youngest girls in the company. She was already preparing to be an officer but did not expect to be given a position of responsibility so soon. She accepted gladly and rushed home after the meeting. Her parents saw the excitement in her face as she took off her coat.

"I'm going to be the cadet leader!" she told them.

Thomas and Emily were pleased.

"You deserve to be chosen," said Emily. "The younger ones love you and you've always helped to look after them."

So now it was Emmie's turn to help organise activities and outings. Trips were made to Wharncliffe Crags and Creswell Crags. She took the girls to paddle at Robin Brook.

105

Only the Boys Brigade was allowed to camp and the girls considered this unfair. So Emmie took them to spend a day at the boys' camp. Her good friend, Lily, who was also a keen member of the brigade, came along to give support. Out in the countryside they could see a tent across the valley. Was that the camp they were seeking? Emmie climbed on an old stone wall and signalled a message in semaphore. The boys answered. Yes, it was the camp! Everyone was hungry when they arrived and packed lunches were devoured quickly. The boys showed them around proudly. Everything inside the tent was shipshape and orderly. The girls were very impressed.

"Let's have a photo," suggested the boys' officer, Harry Ironside.

Everyone gathered round. Edna Dickson came to sit at Emmie's feet. Marie Hault and Joan Beatson squeezed up to Edna. Edna's brother Colin stood at the back.

"Come and sit with us, Lily," called Eva Thompson.

The Houseden twins, Amy and Betty, sat together. Everyone found a place. The older boys lined up in front of their tent, and Don Thompson came rushing up just in time.

"Smile, please!" said Harry.

Afterwards, they had fun exploring their surroundings and playing games. Only too soon, it was time for the girls to leave. It seemed so unfair that the boys could stay and sleep in the tents. Some of the girls had to leave their brothers enjoying

a holiday. Edna and Eva knew that when it was dark their brothers would be singing round the campfire. There were some wistful faces as they set off home but it had been a memorable day. Emmie vowed that one day the girls should be able to camp too.

Emmie was now expected to train the younger girls to take part in the many concerts, a task she enjoyed. She rehearsed Joyce Cooper and Lily Battams in Edna Wolfenden's front room while Edna played the piano. They danced their minuet beautifully but on the first night of the concert Joyce fell over. On the second night, it was Lily's turn to fall down!

"Never mind," consoled Emmie. "There is still tomorrow."

The third and final performance was a success. Joyce and Lily received loud applause. When Emmie's cadets, dressed in white, lined up on the front of the platform, she was very proud of them.

Emmie was also teaching in Sunday school now. Her cousins, Ken and Dougie, were in her class. Aunt Annie threatened the boys.

"If you don't go to Sunday school, there's no dinner!" Emmie was not sure this was the right approach!

Emmie's own training in the Girls Brigade continued at a higher level. Mr Dickson's military experience made him a good leader and he passed on many skills. He taught boys and girls who played in the brigade band to play bugle, trumpet and drums. He trained Emmie and the other seniors in their semaphore signalling, insisting on absolute precision.

Emmie told her parents, "He's a stickler! He makes us repeat times many. Every move we make has to be just right and it's amazing how he can demonstrate with only one arm." She had immense respect for him.

Semaphore signalling, a system of hand-held flags, had been essential in the war and was still recognised as an important skill. Emmie found it fascinating and

worked hard to please Mr Dickson. Her efforts were rewarded when she was selected to take part in a display at the Whitsuntide gathering.

In Emmie's life, the brigade, Sunday school, and church celebrations were all closely interwoven. Whitsuntide was a time when all those connected with the church, old and young, were brought together. It also brought together Christian churches of all denominations. When Emmie was small, she had taken her place with the Sunday school to walk to the great gathering at Norfolk Park. New clothes at Whitsuntide were a tradition and Emmie had always had a new dress. Once in the brigades, she marched in uniform with her company feeling a great sense of pride.

During the weeks leading up to Whitsuntide, churches all around Sheffield resounded with the same wonderful tunes as everyone practised for the big day. Deep Pits was no exception.

In the chapel the choirmaster, Mr Buckland, held his baton poised, and murmured for the umpteenth time, "One more time!" His all-age choir must not disgrace Deep Pits.

At this time, the parade and gathering took place on Whit Mondays, but on some Whit Sundays everyone from Deep Pits assembled to parade up Wulfric Road and round the Manor Estate, pausing to sing the Whitsuntide hymns at regular intervals. It was a good opportunity to prepare for the following day. Then excited children were put to bed early, ready for an early rising and breakfast at the Institute. Each person took his own cup and had potted meat and egg sandwiches. At 7.30 a.m. the senior boys had breakfast, followed by the senior girls at 8.00 a.m. The younger children rushed in at 9.00 a.m., and at 9.30 a.m. everyone assembled for the parade in front of the chapel. The banner was hoisted aloft and every voice was hushed as they saw it fill out in the wind. All the churches had beautiful banners but the people of Deep Pits naturally considered their banner to be the best. Billy Bodsworth and Harry Ironside, both tall youths, were pole-bearers. Two others were chosen to hold the cords, which helped to keep the banner steady. Then the brigade band was arranged behind it. Josh Arnold was at the front with the big drum. He was a real showman! Between dramatic drum rolls and complex rhythms, he twirled his sticks, crossed his arms over his head, threw his sticks into the air and caught them. On one occasion, a stick had to be retrieved from a front garden.

Some of Emmie's cadets played in the band. Maisie Wolfenden and her close friend, Marie Hault, played bugles. Joyce Cooper played a drum. A number of young men played the side-drums. They looked particularly smart in navy caps and jackets with white sashes over one shoulder, which fastened at the hip. The correct term for these was 'haversack'. A leather pouch was attached at the back. This was initially devised to carry a modest ration for expeditions, sports or manoeuvres. Emmie secretly admired dark-haired William Richardson. She thought he wore his cap at a very jaunty angle and watched the two ribbons on it fluttering in the breeze. These ribbons were nicknamed 'follow-me-lads'.

Behind the band came the Girls Brigade flag. This year, Mary Battams had been chosen to carry the flag. This was a great honour and Mary was very conscious of it. The flag was mounted in a leather socket on a strong leather belt.

"I feel so proud I could burst!" Mary confided to Emmie in a whisper.

Emmie followed the flag with her cadets and the rest of the company. Behind them marched the Boys Brigade, their flag flying proudly. The Sunday school children chattered excitedly behind them, admiring new clothes and showing off new shoes. The regular congregation, parents, and friends streamed out at the rear. When this orderly queue was ready, everyone waited impatiently for the people who would be joining them from other, more distant churches. Some of them had a long walk to reach Deep Pits. The children fidgeted as they waited. Emmie told her cadets to listen for the approaching drums.

"Who will be the first to hear them?" she asked. The little girls stood still and concentrated.

"I think I can hear them now," said Edna, her eyes wide with anticipation.

Yes! There was a distant rumble, which swelled into a rhythmic beating, and then the approaching band and the sound of marching feet could be heard. A signal was given. Josh Arnold swung his drumsticks and away they went! Behind the assembled procession of Deep Pits came the congregations of Intake Methodist, Gleadless, and Hollinsend. Together they marched down City Road in a great stream with banners bravely billowing, buglers bugling, the brass instruments gleaming, and the drummers drumming. At the top of Granville Road it was "Left wheel!" and down the hill to the park gates. Those unable to join them gathered on their doorsteps to cheer them on. To see the vast mass of marching people converging on the park with banners and flags so bravely waving was a very moving spectacle. Other processions came to meet them from all directions and waited their turn to enter the park. Mary, carrying her flag, felt a lump in her throat. She felt as if her heart would burst. Emmie's heart was stirred as they passed through the great gates. The children's chattering subsided as they became awe-struck by the enormity of the occasion. Each church paraded beneath the tall avenue of trees to its own roped area. Thousands of people stood on the slopes of the natural amphitheatre of Norfolk Park. There was a great circle of richly coloured banners. In the centre, a dray was parked on which the Salvation Army Band was seated. The Lord Mayor opened the proceedings. Sydney Dyson, with a broad Sheffield accent, introduced the famous

110

conductor, Sir Henry Coward. Sir Henry raised his baton and the Salvation Army struck up a rousing tune. Everyone gave their all. The singing was glorious! Even Mr Buckland was satisfied.

At the conclusion of the Whit Sing came Emmie's big moment. She was one of five girls. One stood in the centre on the dray acting as co-ordinator. Emmie and the other girls were stationed on small platforms at each corner of the gathering on high ground. There was a sudden silence as they stood perfectly still with their white flags ready. Then, in perfect timing, they signalled 'Thank you, Sir Henry'.

Their message was received with tumultuous applause. Emmie gave a sigh of relief.

The day then followed its traditional pattern. The crowd dispersed and all the people returned to their respective churches. At the Institute the Whit Monday lunch was served, and afterwards there were games and races in Farmer Bell's field. John Ironside, the Sunday school superintendent, and Farmer Bell threw sweets across the field and all the children scrambled to find them. The sweets were always boiled sweets. They were spice fish – and unwrapped. No one thought or cared for a moment that Farmer Bell's cows had been grazing in the field that morning! The sweets were the final highlight of a wonderful day.

28. Ice Cream

Emmie dipped her brush in the jam jar of whitewash and concentrated on her artistic efforts. Across the dairy window, in her large script, she wrote:

'Come in, and have a Cooler!'

The day was hot, and Emmie hoped that people passing by would be prompted into buying a penny cornet. Her mother's ice cream was well-known locally and is still remembered today with nostalgia. It was made of fresh custard and flavoured with fresh seasonal fruit. Emily generally made ice cream in the summer, but also for special occasions or if there was a glut of milk.

Of course, Deep Pits Dairy had no refrigerator and so Thomas had to buy ice. On Saturdays, the milk round finished at the Shrewsbury Alms Houses in the Park District. Nearby, on the corner between South Street and Granville Street, was the Ice Company. Trams now run along Granville Street, and all the houses and shops are gone. Thomas bought a one hundredweight block of ice wrapped in hessian and heaved it into the cart. The ice would keep the ice cream cool for a week.

One hot summer's day, the family was sitting around the table having their midday meal. Emmie, who had been thoughtfully staring into space, suddenly said, "You know, if we could only deliver ice cream like we deliver the milk, we should sell much more." She laughed at her own suggestion and everyone joined in.

"Ice cream for breakfast!" said Evelyn.

Thomas looked at Emmie.

"Your idea is not as daft as it sounds," he said. "People do sell ice cream from horse-drawn carts. The problem is that we are all fully occupied already and the horses work hard enough as it is."

"Never mind," said Emmie, jokingly. "I'll take it round in a wheelbarrow!"

They laughed again, but Thomas put his head on one side and said, "Actually, that's not such a daft idea. We could have a proper handcart made. Now that the Manor Estate is growing, there would be trade around the houses there." Everybody pondered this suggestion.

"Someone would have to take the cart round," Thomas commented.

"I could do that!" offered Emmie eagerly.

"No daughter of mine will push a cart round the streets," said Thomas firmly. "Besides, your mother needs you here. In any case, there is no cart ready."

After some discussion together, Thomas and Emily decided to have a handcart made. It was very attractive when completed, painted in yellow and green, with 'Deep Pits Dairy' in bold letters on each side.

Thomas was intending to sell the ice cream during the school holidays. He was wondering whom to employ and Emmie said, "Mrs Garrett came into the shop this morning and told Mum that Mr Garrett is still looking for regular work."

"The very chap," said Thomas.

The Garretts were good neighbours and Thomas felt they deserved better opportunities. Both Mr and Mrs Garrett had served in the First World War. Mrs Garrett had been in the Women's Royal Flying Corps at Coal Aston – a huge place – where wooden planes were repaired and fabric glued to their wings. Mr Garrett rarely spoke of his experiences but they knew he had joined up at the age of sixteen and been sent to France. He had been in fierce fighting and buried in a shell hole for two days before being discovered. He had survived but was left profoundly deaf. Money was short and they were grateful to buy the cracked eggs sold very cheaply at the dairy.

Mr Garrett was very happy to become an ice cream man and Emmie's little friend Dorothy was delighted to be going with her father. She knew she could help him if he had difficulties because he could not hear.

Thomas fitted the ice cream tub into its compartment and packed the ice around it. Away they went on their first sales trip.

Dorothy was very excited when they returned. While Mr Garrett counted the takings with Thomas, she chatted to Emmie.

"We sold it all!" Her eyes grew large. "Lots of people came and Dad had to make cornets quickly." Then she whispered to Emmie, "When it was all gone, I was allowed to scrape it out!"

So everyone benefited from this arrangement, and it helped the Garretts a little at a difficult time. Eventually Mr Garrett became a grinder and did very well at his trade.

Meanwhile, Emmie was becoming efficient in all the daily tasks. She had mastered handling the horse and the milk float, and could be trusted to take them out on longer errands. There was only one mishap, when Firefly stumbled and fell. Emmie was thrown into the bottom of the cart. Shaken, she rushed to Firefly. Fortunately, apart from a cut leg, the pony was unhurt. She tried to bandage the leg with her handkerchief but it was not big enough.

Emmie's favourite errand was to Ford where she could buy extra eggs from several farms. The countryside was beautiful and Emmie felt content and truly independent as they trotted along. This was the life! Thomas, noting Emmie's confidence in handling the pony, decided that the time had come to let her venture further. He suggested that she should take the ice cream tub to the Norton Show. Emmie was thrilled. Clad in her spotless white overall, with the float packed with all that was necessary, she set off for the showground. She was not alone on this journey. Many farmers were taking trucks of livestock to show or sell at this famous agricultural event. Gleaming and decorated horses and horse-drawn vehicles of all kinds were heading in the same direction. Several times a charabanc overtook her. She felt a sense of achievement as she drove through the entrance and found a pitch beneath a tree where she and the pony could have some shade. Having set out the ice cream scoop and made sure that all was to hand, Emmie picked up her small handbell and shook it.

"Ice cream!" she called, self-consciously. "Ice cream!"

At first there were not many customers, but as the afternoon wore on and the temperature rose, people began to ask, "Where did you buy your ice cream?" and soon Emmie had a steady queue. There were many familiar faces from Deep Pits, which made Emmie feel at home. After a while there was a lull, and Emmie took the opportunity to make sure that Firefly had a drink. While she was busy, a voice called, "Shop!" and someone rang her bell. She turned to see a young man smiling at her.

"Hello, Emmie," he said.

"Hello, Billy," she responded, flushing a little. Emmie knew Billy Richardson's family well, but she had not had much contact with Billy. He went to chapel but he was two years older and moved in a different circle. She knew he was a good tennis player and she had seen him playing billiards, but Emmie was not sporty and had given little thought to him. Looking at him now, she remembered how smart he had looked in his Boys Life Brigade uniform playing a drum.

"Have you any cornets left?" he asked, and she climbed up into the float to serve him. She made sure that he had a big scoop of ice cream and, as she passed it to him, she was aware of a special moment between them. Emmie expected that he would return to his friends but he stayed to chat and soon she felt quite at ease with him.

The time flew by and the ice cream disappeared. Emmie knew, regretfully, that she would have to go home. Billy helped her clear away and walked alongside her to the big gateway.

"See you on Sunday at chapel," he said as she halted the float to say goodbye.

"Yes, I'll be there," she replied and felt as though they had both made a promise.

When she arrived home her parents saw her glowing cheeks and bright eyes.

"A day in the fresh air has done you good," they said.

Emmie agreed. Not only her cheeks were glowing. Her heart was glowing too.

29. All the Fun of the Fair!

Sunday came. Emmie went to church morning and evening and taught Sunday school in the afternoon. At the evening service, she sat with the choir where she could see Billy Richardson in his seat at the back of the church. She concentrated on the preacher and the hymns and tried not to look in his direction.

When the service was over, Emmie dutifully greeted friends and relations before gathering outside with a crowd of her own age – the 'crush'. Her cousin, Norah, and her close friends, Lily and Gladys, were waiting. Soon, Doug Austin, Bob Taylor and Arnold Precious joined them. During the mirth and merriment that ensued Emmie was aware that Billy Richardson was close by, in deep conversation with a group of his own friends.

There was some larking about and then Doug Austin said, "Come on, then. Let's be off!" and they all turned to walk up City Road on their usual evening stroll.

Emmie felt a pang of disappointment but set off with the others.

As they moved away a voice behind them called, "Can anybody come?" It was Billy. Emmie's heart leapt!

Her good-natured friend Lily said, "Yes, walk with us," and moved over so that he could walk between them.

Their conversation was as light as their spirits as they made a round walk, wandering along Spring Lane and returning down City Road in the twilight.

Norah, who was now living in Don Terrace with her family, and Lily called, "Goodnight" and disappeared down their passages. Gladys and the other boys continued on their way home. Billy stood with Emmie at the end of her passage.

"Tomorrow is Bank Holiday Monday," he said. "Would you like to come out with me?"

"I'd love to," replied Emmie honestly, and they smiled at each other.

He touched her hand briefly. "See you tomorrow."

At Wulfric Road he turned and waved. Emmie waved back.

The following morning, Emmie helped her mother and was free to meet Billy in the afternoon. The rain fell but was not noticed. There was so much to talk about. After exploring the Botanical Gardens in Sheffield they found a bench in a sheltered corner. First, they talked about the farm and the coming harvest. Billy was enthralled by the threshing machine and took every opportunity to see it working.

Emmie wanted to know more about Billy.

"You work at the pit," she said.

He nodded. "Yes, like my father, my grandfather and all the other men in my family."

"It must be very dangerous," commented Emmie.

Billy laughed at her serious face. "When all the safety rules are followed there is not much to fear, but accidents can happen. 1923 was a bad year. Nine men lost their lives in local collieries and many men were injured." Billy told Emmie that his father had been a member of the Rotherham Rescue Team. This was a specially trained group that operated over a wide area and was called out in the most dangerous situations. Emmie thought of his kind and gentle father.

"I didn't know he was so brave," she said.

"He was a very fit man," said Billy and she recognised a note of anxiety in his voice. "He is not so well now," Billy confided. "Sometimes he can hardly breathe at nights – too much coal dust."

"Did he want you to go into the pit?" asked Emmie.

"Well, when I left school in 1923 there were not many jobs. Dad was pleased because I was lucky enough to become an apprentice blacksmith. That meant I was not only learning a skilled trade but that I spend most of my time on the surface."

"I thought blacksmiths made horseshoes," said Emmie. "You have ponies in the pit, don't you?"

"Yes, we have ponies in the pit but I don't work with them. One of the lads does. He has to start his shift earlier to make sure all the horses are properly shod before the miners start their shift."

"So what do you do?" enquired Emmie.

"I make or repair anything made of metal. Actually, I've just finished a big job. I've just made a complete set of chains for the pit cage." Emmie sensed his excitement and was proud to share it.

"It felt good to mark them with my initials and the year," he said. Emmie looked impressed.

Billy gazed directly at her and said firmly, "I'm qualified now but I'm not always going to be a blacksmith. I've already started night school and one day I'll be an engineer." Emmie believed him and they continued discussing hopes and dreams.

(Had they been able to see into the future, they would have been amazed to see their son, like his father, an apprentice at the pit, wire-brushing a set of chains in the chain room under the supervision of one George Trout. And as the initials 'W.R.', and '1930' became visible, they would have heard George say, "Look, Eric, your father made these chains!")

But Emmie and Billy were only momentarily concerned with the future on that day in the Botanical Gardens. Their present was much more interesting. Billy took her hand and they wandered off to have some tea. Later they went to the theatre to see 'Tons of Money'. All good days come to an end but there were many more to come for Emmie and Billy.

The next Saturday night they enjoyed a jaunt to the fair. They played hoop-la and Billy had a go on the rifle range. Emmie loved the galloping horses and coaxed him to ride with her. There was a small circus, and inside the Big Top they sat close together. The darkened tent was airless and the smell of sawdust was all round them. They laughed at the clowns, admired the horses, and felt sorry for the few wild animals. When they emerged from this exotic atmosphere the night was darker and the fairground lights brighter. A crowd of burly young men was gathered, and at its centre was a booth outside which a large placard issued an invitation to 'Test Your Strength'. Emmie and Billy watched for a while as, one after another, the young men picked up the hammer and slammed it down on the base of a machine similar to a weighing machine. A tall, numbered scale attached to the back was topped by a painted, cheeky-faced Scotsman wearing a kilt. The aim was to apply such force that a disc bounced up the scale, under the kilt, and rang a bell.

There was some arrogant laughter and a spirit of aggressive rivalry as each youth tried to beat the highest score. No one rang the bell. Emmie found herself horrified when Billy suddenly decided to test his strength. He stepped forward to pay and there was a raucous laugh from the crowd. Billy was not tall and definitely lightweight, being less than eight stones. He was just about to pick up the hammer when he remembered that he was wearing his watch. He stopped, removed it and passed it to Emmie. This gesture convulsed the crowd. They fell about, clutching each other with mirth.

A rough voice shouted, "Go on, then. Thee try an' pick it up!" There was more harsh laughter, but this time it stopped as Billy lifted the big hammer as if it were a feather brush. He swung the hammer with practised ease. Almost simultaneously the bell rang loud and clear. The crowd was silenced. Some of the youths had not believed that the bell ever functioned. The stallholder, revelling in his increased takings, offered Billy a free turn. Happy to oblige him, Billy repeated his success. Heads turned, mouths dropped open, and people stared as they walked away arm in arm. Billy replaced his watch and Emmie exclaimed, "How did you do that?"

Billy grinned. "It's my job," he said simply. "I do it every day."

Emmie always said that Billy was her hero.

That night, the 16th August 1930, she wrote in her diary 'Billy Richardson is much nicer than I thought he was."

30. HIGHS AND LOWS

"Well done!" said Emmie enthusiastically.

Billy smirked. "I've been practising!" he said.

Emmie had been teaching Billy to play the piano for several months and he had just reached the end of 'Swiss Air' without a mistake. Any spare time they had was spent together. Billy brought his night school homework to do in Emmie's front room, and if this was finished in time he had a piano lesson. His piano playing was not a lasting occupation but it provided him with an opportunity to sit close to Emmie on the piano stool. Emmie was not highly accomplished but she liked to play and had a very light touch. Billy loved to listen to her and occasionally bought her some sheet music for her collection. Emmie and Billy had already formed a strong bond which was to last all their lives. In the 1930s this constancy kept Emmie strong as many things around her were changing.

One big change had already taken place. Her grandparents had moved out of the old farmhouse. Their son, Walter, had moved in with his wife and their children, Walter, Ronnie, Kenny, Dougie, Eileen and Gerald. Eileen, seeking a change from the rough and tumble of her brothers, frequently visited her Aunt Emily and Uncle Thomas across the road. She knew Emmie would tell her stories.

Farmer Bell was seventy-three when he retired. He found leaving the farm very hard and the move distressed him. Farming had been a complete way of life for him. Fortunately his daughter, Ada, welcomed both her parents into her home at 611 Don Terrace. Ada had, after many years, divorced her husband whose bouts of heavy drinking had made him violent. Emmie's mother was both relieved and happy to have the sister she loved so close, and Emmie was delighted to see her cousins, Norah, Teddy and Barbara every day. Barbara was three years old, a pretty, dark-haired child who became a playmate for Eileen. Emmie loved both little girls and told them stories. During the next few years, all these cousins grew to know each other well and had many happy times together. Ada must have found it hard to care for her parents as well as her three children, but Thomas, Emily and Emmie helped as much as they could.

Grandad was never the same after being uprooted from the farm, and Emmie ran round to see them nearly every day. On the 6th June 1931, Walter Bell fell ill. His family watched him anxiously but his condition deteriorated rapidly. Emmie took her turn to sit with Grandad through the night. He slept fitfully, flushed and hot. Emmie held his hand and thought what an important part he had played in her life. He stirred and struggled to speak. She moved closer to him.

He recognised her and whispered urgently, "Don't forget to feed the calves, Emmie. You must feed the calves!"

"I'll feed the calves, Grandad," Emmie promised. "I won't forget." She squeezed his hand and his head settled more peacefully on the pillow. His eyes closed. There had not been calves for a long time at the farm but her promise had consoled him. Those were the last words Grandad spoke to Emmie. He died on the 10th June.

Grandad's funeral was on the following Saturday. Emmie was impressed by the quiet dignity of her Grandma as the whole family assembled. Four black Belgian stallions stood ready to carry Walter Bell on his last journey. The driver, in his black top hat, noticed Emmie's young cousin, nine-year-old Kenny Bell, looking at the handsome team of horses. He asked the youngster if he would like to sit by his side. Emmie thought that that would have pleased her grandfather and Kenny never forgot his place of honour in the procession.

Walter Bell had been well-known and well loved at Deep Pits, but Emmie was amazed how many people had made their way to the cemetery. Hundreds of people had gathered to pay their last respects at his burial. It was a sad day but Emmie knew Grandad had enjoyed a long and active life. Her life was in front of her and she looked forward to sharing it with Billy. Plans had been made for her to join his parents, Alice and Newell, for a week at Scarborough in August. Emmie was twenty, and a week at the seaside with Billy was an exciting prospect. She and her mother made a shopping excursion to Sheffield for a new suitcase – the first she had ever had – a pair of pyjamas, and some material for a new dress.

Billy collected her early on the 1st August and they caught the eight o'clock bus, arriving at two o'clock. They were greeted by sunshine, and walked on the harbour without coats. After tea they went to Peasholm and Scalby. Riding back to Scarborough on the miniature railway, Emmie and Billy felt very contented.

During that week they explored the castle, visited the Singing Shops and Gala Land. Emmie stored up romantic memories of dancing in the Olympia ballroom and tea for two in the Cosy Café while watching a rough sea crashing on the rocks. A highlight of the week was a Royal visit. Scarborough was spruced up and decorated with bunting for this auspicious occasion. Thunder rolled and heavy rain fell shortly before the proceedings but did not deter great crowds of people gathering to see the arrival of Princess Mary. The princess had travelled from Bridlington where she had launched a new lifeboat during the morning. That ceremony had been cut short due to rain.

In Scarborough, where another lifeboat waited to be launched, they were more fortunate. Alice and Newell had found a good place to observe the proceedings but Emmie was standing on tiptoe.

"She's coming!" said Alice, and Emmie cried, "Where? Where?"

Billy crouched down and said, "Climb on my shoulders." Emmie hurried to do so and Billy stood up carefully. Now her view was wonderful. A splendid contingent of the Royal Horse Guards held their trumpets aloft. A glorious fanfare greeted Princess Mary as she approached with the local dignitaries. She looked very regal in an elegant hat. She walked slowly along the line of the Church Lads Brigade and the Girl Guides. The lifeboat men, smart in uniform, were lined up awaiting her presence. The band played. In the centre, the new lifeboat, its paintwork gleaming, was positioned for the launch. The crowd cheered as Princess Mary took her place and then there was silence.

The Princess made a short speech concluding with "I name this boat *Herbert Joy 11*." She broke a bottle of champagne across the bows of the boat. Then came the long-awaited moment. Princess Mary was handed an ornate pair of scissors. With a smile and a wave for the crowd she cut the red, white and blue ribbon and the new lifeboat slid gracefully into the sea. It was a grand sight. Perched on Billy's shoulders, Emmie felt on top of the world!

31. TIME DOESN'T STAND STILL

Soon after Grandad Bell died, his son, Walter, began making some changes on the farm. The stack yard was exposed to the cold winds that blew across the open fields. Walter and his sons raised the wall to a height of twelve feet, giving better shelter to the livestock. Emmie was not sure that she wanted the farm to change but, as her father said, "Time doesn't stand still."

Changes were taking place all around. Electricity came to Don Terrace! That was very convenient. Thomas, with an eye to the future, invested in a motorcar. This was an Overland. For a long time, the only car around Deep Pits was a Studebaker driven by Marie Hault's father. He was a chauffeur and the car was kept in Grooby's yard. Marie was the envy of all the local children because she was sometimes to be seen in the front seat. Emmie suspected that one day the Overland would be used for milk deliveries. Already her father used it to fetch milk from surrounding farms.

Meanwhile life went on very much as usual. Emmie and Billy had a big circle of friends and with the social life of Deep Pits Institute, a round of dances, socials and concerts, life was never dull. The cinema was a popular and affordable treat. Emmie's cousin Norah was now courting. Emmie, Billy, Norah and Norman often went out together.

To surprise Emmie, Billy ordered a gramophone and it was duly delivered. Emmie looked at it in awe.

"It's beautiful!" she breathed.

The shining wooden cabinet had a lid that lifted to reveal the velvet-covered turntable and the heavy, shining, metal head that held the needle in position. A special compartment held a small tin box that contained spare needles. A velvet pad to clean the records fitted neatly into its corner. In the cupboard below were two shelves to hold records. On one side of the cabinet was the winding handle. Billy had several records. He took one from its cover, polished it with the velvet pad and laid it on the turntable with exaggerated formality. Assuming the air of a magician, he wound the handle round and round, lifted the arm and the record began to spin. The needle was lowered and music floated out. The sweet tones of Florrie Ford drifted into the room – 'When you're smiling…'. They listened ecstatically and then laughed hysterically as it wound down, reducing the song to a drunken dirge. The gramophone was very popular. Emmie and Billy often had their friends round for a musical evening.

The Life Brigade continued to play a part in their lives although Billy's shift work interfered with all his activities. They both became corporals and had medals inscribed with their names. Emmie's had three bars attached for Good Service in 1930, 1931 and 1932.

In 1932, Emmie was twenty-one. Her mother offered to give her a party.

Emmie declined.

"I'm not fussy about a party but" – she hesitated – "I should like to invite all my family and friends to my wedding." That satisfied her mother. She knew that Emmie and Billy were not planning to marry immediately.

"You shall have a lovely wedding," she promised Emmie.

That year, Emmie and Billy went on holiday with his parents again. This time they went to Morecambe. The weather was wonderful and they swam every day. Emmie and Billy scrambled over to a rocky

headland. The water there was deep and fairly calm. In between dips, they sat on the rocks and looked across at Billy's parents who waved frantically. Billy and Emmie carried on diving and jumping into the sea. When they returned Newell pointed to a notice that read: 'Caution! This water is forty feet deep'.

Emmie said to Billy, "I thought it seemed a long time coming up!"

This holiday was the last they shared with his parents. Newell's health began to fail. He had several spells in sanatoria.

Other anxieties followed over the next two years. The building of the Arbourthorne Estate began, and it grieved Emmie and her family to see the fields her grandfather had tended hidden by roads and houses. The Manor Estate had already taken much of the land and now the rest of the farm fields were going. Everyone agreed they were glad Farmer Bell had not lived to see it happen. Thomas, seeing the writing on the wall, decided sadly that the horses would have to go. Emmie pleaded but realized that all their circumstances were changing. Thomas bought an Austin Seven van for milk deliveries. It was a tremendously sad day for Emmie and her family when the horses were led away. It nearly broke Emmie's heart.

Her Uncle Walter had no option but to leave the farm and to find work elsewhere. Many of the people who moved into the new houses had come from city streets and had little understanding of the countryside. The beautiful Buck Woods, which stood beyond the farm fields, were ravaged. The yellowhammers, which sang so sweetly there, flew away and never returned. Fortunately, not all the newcomers were so inclined and some families joined Deep Pits Methodist Church. They were welcomed with open arms.

Emmie and Billy were relieved to find that no houses were built behind Billy's home. Instead, a school was built at a distance and the field remained to serve the school. Emmie and Billy, like other occupants of the long row of houses, could still sit on the garden wall and dangle their legs over the field. One day as they sat there, sharing a plate of sandwiches, Billy spoke seriously to Emmie.

"I think I've found a house that would be just right for us."

Emmie's eyes lit up.

"Where?" she asked. "Not too far away?" They had been looking round for a house for some time. Billy was determined they would have a home of their own.

"It's at Intake," he told her. "They are only just laying foundations."

"Can we go and look?" asked Emmie.

"What are we waiting for?" smiled Billy.

So it came about that a very excited Emmie and Billy put a deposit on number thirty, Newlands Avenue. They walked regularly to Intake to watch it grow. Their future home cost £215 and the mortgage was fifteen shillings per week. Now Emmie and Billy began to save even more seriously. They fixed a date for their wedding. Thomas and Emily began to make plans. Emily dreamed about the food she would provide for her daughter's wedding. There would be a feast to remember.

Amid all this excitement, Emmie and Billy discussed a private concern. Billy's father's chest complaint was worsening. Would he live long enough to be with them on their wedding day? They could only pray that he would.

32. A Day to Remember

Emmie sat up in bed and looked round the familiar room. How well it had sheltered her for more than twenty years. Tomorrow she would be married and this bed would be empty. There had been so many plans and preparations made over the last few months that there had been little time to dwell on being uprooted from her family home. The invitations had been sent out long ago and every day the mail brought responses. Emmie wondered why the Walkers, who now lived in Manchester, had only just replied.

"Still," she thought, "it was a lovely letter." She read again:

Dear Emmie,

It was a pleasure to recognise the writing on the envelope just received. What a pleasing surprise. June16th; so near, there is scarcely time to anticipate the day. We should have been glad to have been present and must be content to be with you in tender thought and good wishes. On Saturday I am presiding at an open air event; a Rose Queen Carnival. But the real queen will be at Talbot Street and holding her reception at Deep Pits. You and yours will have the felicitations of a countless company, many you will not see, but they will be with you. May your families have increasing joy in your marriage. It is a big day for your mother and we know that you will be her girl all the more when you bring your husband into the family circle as a son added to the family. I am very pleased to hear how well Mr Stoparde is getting on amongst you all and can congratulate him upon presiding on the occasion of your marriage. For you and your husband-to-be, may June be golden, in precious

associations, and we would follow you upon life's pilgrim journey
with prayerful desires for increasing prosperity and blessing. We
write in every good wish to you and yours,
As ever your sincere friends
Wm. and S. Walker

"People are so kind," Emmie thought, remembering countless little parcels passed to her on the milk round. She pondered, with a thrill, on the house at Newlands Road. The kitchen cupboards were already packed with glass and china. The bed was prepared with new sheets, blankets, eiderdown, and bolster. Norah and Norman had bought them an electric stove with artificial coal and a revolving fan that produced very lifelike flames. The Girls Life Brigade had presented her with Art Ware bookends. Her cadets had given her a jade and silver ashtray. Neither she nor Billy smoked but it would come in useful for visitors. Billy's sister Dolly – her real name was Rose but it was never used – and her husband Ernest had bought them a wooden dinner wagon. Ernest, who was clever with his hands, had made them a clock. The dial and mechanism had been part of the dashboard of a car and he had set it into a well-shaped piece of wood. Emmie smiled as she thought of it ticking away on the mantelpiece.

"Ernest is so kind and funny," thought Emmie. "He will be a good best man tomorrow."

It seemed strange that Ernest should have married Dolly, who had a rather sharp tongue if the truth were known. Thinking of Dolly brought to mind the dresses hanging downstairs in the front room. The four grown-up bridesmaids had dresses in mauve floral georgette. Emmie had chosen a pattern with a small cape but neither Dolly nor Emmie's cousin Frances liked the cape design. Their dresses would be without the capes. Emmie hoped these temperamental ladies would not squabble with each other!

"Thank goodness," Emmie sighed, "for Norah and Lily." They loved the dresses with the fashionable capes.

Her thoughts were interrupted as the old sheepdog stirred and stood up beside her. He rested his head on the bedcover and Emmie felt a sudden pang at leaving him. She rubbed his ears and a tear dropped on to his nose. He seemed to know that she was going.

"I'm not going very far, Jack," she told him. "I shall be back to see you often."

She climbed out of bed to switch off the light and in the near-dark saw the white, floaty dress hanging on the wardrobe door. She thought of Billy on his last night at home too. She felt a great rush of love for him and an immediate longing to be with him. Tomorrow they would be together forever. Emmie laid her head on the pillow and went to sleep.

The following morning passed in a blur of excitement for Emmie. Visitors came bearing parcels of all shapes and sizes and Emmie felt quite overcome by such generosity and affection. The postman wished her 'every happiness' as he placed a stack of cards into her hands. There was scarcely time for a bite of breakfast or lunch. Bill's Aunty brought her son, Donald, to be changed into his satin pageboy's suit. The bridesmaids began to arrive. Emmie retreated upstairs to dress. The precious white silk stockings were pulled on with extreme care and held in place by a pair of fancy new garters. These were trimmed with blue ribbons and rosebuds. Norah and Lily came up to help her. They admired the pretty garters and slipped the white georgette dress over her head very carefully. While Norah held the long veil of Brussels net in place, Lily secured it with a Juliet cap of orange blossoms and pearls.

"You look lovely!" they said.

"You look lovely too," said Emmie. For a few seconds, the three close friends felt suspended in the sensation that nothing would ever be the same again.

Thomas and Emily came in wearing their wedding finery. Their eyes glowed when they saw Emmie. To them she was the perfect bride. They all trooped downstairs and Emmie gave Barbara and Eileen their posies. They looked very pretty in mint-green dresses and headdresses of small flowers. Soon the bridesmaids were whisked away and Emily gave her daughter a kiss and departed too. Emmie watched through the window as the large shining car appeared. It had been ordered from Abbots. Emmie's Grandma Bell was to drive to church with Emmie and her father.

As Grandma was led, smiling, to the luxurious car, Thomas turned to Emmie. "We shan't be locking the door," he said. "Remember, Emmie, you always have a home here."

They drove in stately fashion to Talbot Street Methodist Church (Deep Pits had no licence for marriages). Here Emmie found, to her astonishment, a Guard of Honour from the Girls Life Brigade. The girls and their officers were lined up smartly and wore the triumphant smiles of those who have long kept a secret safely. Her cousin Jack, proud to be an usher, opened the inner door and her retinue of bridesmaids and pageboy gathered behind her. The organ played. Emmie strained to see Billy. He turned his head to smile at her and she knew everything was going to be alright. Another face stood out in the crowd as she neared the altar. Billy's father was here! The previous day the family had been unsure whether he would be allowed out of the sanatorium. Their eyes met briefly in happy recognition and then she was standing by Billy's side.

Emmie and Billy were married reverently and tenderly by the Reverend Stoparde. They made their vows clearly and confidently. All went according to plan and they emerged joyfully to be smothered in confetti.

They were driven back up City Road, waving to clusters of people standing at the end of their passages hoping to catch a glimpse of the bride. Emmie and Billy felt like royalty. At the chapel, where everything lay ready for the reception, they received another tumultuous welcome.

Photographs, speeches, the cutting of the wedding cake, and all that is customary on a wedding day followed their arrival at Deep Pits. Eventually, Emmie and Billy were taken to the station to catch a train to Blackpool where they were to spend their honeymoon with Aunty Edie and Uncle Sam in their boarding house. There, they were welcomed rapturously by Emmie's cousin Joy who rushed out to

hug them both. Aunt Edie and Uncle Sam stood in the doorway, smiling broadly. Joy took the suitcase from Billy. He put his arm round Emmie as they walked up the path. Their life together had begun.

*   *   *   *   *

134

The real flavour of the day was recalled in the letters written soon after the event. A letter from Billy's father arrived two days later:

> *Dear Son and Daughter,*
> *Just a line to say I received your card all right and glad you arrived*
> *safe. Well I hope you had a good time and glad to say I feel pretty*
> *well this morning, did not have a good night on Saturday, no doubt*
> *due to the extra exertion of the day. Well Billy take care of her and*
> *Emmie take care of him and you will not go far wrong... I am glad*
> *everything went off all right for it was a wedding and no mistake –*
> *something for Deep Pits to remember. I must now close.*
> *Wishing you much happiness and love*
> *From your loving Dad*

Newell wrote again next day:

> *...Well I don't think you could have a more pleasant day than*
> *Saturday from 3 p.m. as I thought it was very good and I wished I*
> *could have stopped to see the finish at the station. I bet they thought*

*you had all gone mad and not much need to put on cases 'just
married' as I bet they could see that. Well please remember me to
Uncle Sam and Aunt Edith. Don't forget as we're all one family
now.*

Alice added her own postscript:

*Well dears, just made your curtains but I will leave them for you
to fix. Went up Monday and Wednesday, took your clothes Billy. Mr
Evans says he will have to take cart with yours Emmie. Been to
your mums three times this week. It bucked them up.*

Emmie and Billy were only away for a week's honeymoon but correspondence
flowed both ways. Aunt Ada sent them a postcard:

*Pleased you are having a happy time, hope it will continue
throughout your lives. Your Ma and Dad are champion.*

Emmie loved Aunt Edie who was more like an older sister than an aunt. Edie was
jolly, full of life and always laughing. Emmie was pleased to meet up again with

her younger cousin, Joycelyn, who was a dancer at Blackpool Tower. Emmie and Billy went to watch her and thought it was a very glamorous performance. Edie was thrilled to have Emmie and Billy to stay. Her only sadness was that, while she had been preparing for their visit and caring for other guests, she had missed the wedding celebrations. Her sister, Ada, wrote to try to compensate for this disappointment:

> *Dear Edie and all*
>
> *Many thanks for the post card received this morning. Yes, I can guess you are pleased to have the newly-weds with you and I'm sure they couldn't be with anyone better for the first week of their married life. What a grand time they must be having. I hope the honeymoon will continue all their lives. They are a lovely pair and how grand they did look on Saturday. Yes, I did wish you could have been there too. Everything went on beautifully. Our Emmie looked lovely, just as you did at eighteen – image – so that is a compliment to you both and a true one. Oh love I could tell you lots of lovely things about the wedding and the people there. Our Mother was dressed up nice and went in a carriage with Emmie. They looked lovely. Mother was champion all the time. Our Willie made some grand speeches and several more besides. Food and drink – it was one continual gorge. Fancy apples and oranges, toffees, cigarettes, cigars and wines. I was kept at it all the time serving and so was our Emily. She was busy as well. Nobody went short and everybody wished Evans had another daughter. Some said that if that was how they sent a daughter off what would it have been for a son... Barbara and Eileen had a good time and looked very nice. The dresses in mauve were lovely. Norah is having hers shortened this week. Well love my wrist is tired and its dinnertime and nowt ready. Your loving sister, Ada.*

Alice wrote again:

Dear Emmie and Billy,

Glad you are having a good time. Have a good rest and come back as brown as berries. Don't go to too many dances! Well dears we had a splendid time when you had gone. Mr Pemburton was a grand help, never flagged until closing time, a time never to be forgotten by Deep Pits folk. We finished up with Auld Lang Syne right round the room. It was hardly big enough to hold them all. Dad was a little tired yesterday. I took the nurses a piece of cake. They were pleased. There is a good account of it in the Independent, must save you one. Called in at your Mum and Dads to look at presents, stayed and had a glass of wine and bucked Mum up a little. Dad says he pushed open your bedroom door – he forgot. It will take a bit of getting used to.

With love from Mum.

Emmie and Billy enjoyed reading these accounts on their honeymoon in Blackpool, and Emmie saved them. She re-read them many times. She kept them with other precious mementoes in an old envelope. Their wedding day had certainly been a day to remember.

33. Life Couldn't Be Better

mmie and Billy were very happy in their new home, not too far from their parents. They visited them frequently and still attended church at Deep Pits. It was hard to watch Billy's father, this once-active man, deteriorate day by day. He had been captain of the cricket team, a member of the football team and skilled in many aspects of work. He had met the arduous demands of the Rotherham Rescue Team. Sadly, pneumoconiosis – the collier's disease – had attacked his lungs and his days were limited.

Newell was fifty-two years old when he died in November 1934 and the whole family felt his loss deeply. Alice was not left alone because her daughter Dolly and her husband Ernest had made their home with Billy's parents. Emmie and Billy consoled themselves with the thought that he had lived to see them married. A few months later, their delight in finding that Emmie was expecting their first baby was tempered by sadness. Newell would never see their children. Alice, bravely determined to be positive, pointed out that the new baby would be a great comfort to her and rejoiced in the coming of her first grandchild. On 20th August 1935, after a frighteningly difficult labour, Emmie gave birth to a baby boy. His name had already been decided. Since Emmie's parents had lost their only son in infancy, the new baby would be christened Evans to carry on the family name. He became Eric Evans Richardson. The midwife weighed him with bags of sugar and declared him to be ten pounds and two Oxos. Emmie was overjoyed but, in her absorption with her baby, did not realise that her family was holding back tragic news until she was stronger. A few days before, her small cousin, Barbara, had been suddenly taken ill with an ear infection, developing mastoiditis from which she had died. Billy found it hard to break such dreadful news. Emmie could not believe that the little girl who had been so thrilled to be her bridesmaid the previous year had been taken from them. She wept for her and for her Aunt Ada. She knew how much Norah and Teddy would be grieving for their sister. Emmie felt such conflicting emotions – so much happiness and so much heartbreak.

Nevertheless, the new baby was welcomed with great joy and many good wishes by family and friends. Emmie kept the letter from the minister, Reverend Stoparde, who had married them.

He wrote:

...we hope you will soon be well again so you may fully realise the glorious joy of the treasure that has come to you.

It was just as well that they could not realise the extent of their talented treasure's determination, or foresee his alarming escapades! But that was all in the future and Emmie revelled in her motherhood. Billy adored them both and they were very contented. In June 1936 there was another addition to the family. Dolly and Ernest became parents too and Alice had two grandsons. The new baby was christened Neil.

140

Around this time another milestone was passed. Billy gained his Ordinary National Certificate. Fitting studies around shift work had never been easy. He had left school in the difficult days of 1923 at the age of fourteen and started work in short trousers. This was the first academic achievement in the family. His hard work was beginning to show dividends. When the results came, Emmie's eyes shone. She wound her arms round his neck.

"I'm so proud of you!" she told him.

A friend of Billy's also considered him to be an up-and-coming young man and suggested that Billy join him in selling insurance. There seemed to be some advantages in this option. There would be no more shift work, more time for his family, and good possibilities for promotion.

"What do you think?" Billy asked Emmie.

"You must make up your own mind," Emmie answered.

Secretly, remembering Newell's ill health and the dangers of accidents at the pit, she was tempted to persuade him into this clean and safe work. Billy decided to apply and was taken on. There was one main obstacle. The Prudential Company insisted that their operators lived within a certain boundary. Reluctantly, Emmie and Billy sold their house and bought one on Tylney Road. This was close to Granville Road and not far from Manor Lane School, which they had both attended. Emmie liked to think that Eric could follow in their footsteps at Manor Lane. Billy was very successful in his new work but they did not settle in their new surroundings. Their first house had been new. This house was much older and had no bathroom. It seemed dark and Emmie, who had always dismissed the idea of ghosts, actually wondered if it was haunted. Time passed and, although Billy was doing well, he realised he had no satisfaction in his work. Emmie recognised his lack of enthusiasm and together they faced the fact that his heart was not in his work.

When Billy decided to return to the pit his employers at the Prudential offered him promotion, but Billy's mind was made up and Emmie supported his choice.

"You always said you wanted to be an engineer," she reminded him. They were both thankful when he was able to return to his old job.

Not far away, new houses were being built. Several side-roads were being created leading off the other side of Granville Road. Granville Road was very steep and a main route into Sheffield. The houses being built on Essex Road, the highest side-road, had a good view across Sheffield and the surrounding hills. Emmie and

Billy went to inspect Essex Road. Number twenty-two attracted them and they became the first occupants. To their delight, they were once again close neighbours of the Dickson family. As soon as they moved in, they felt at home. This was the beginning of a happy time. Eric was progressing rapidly and fast became a chatterbox. He was idolised by his grandparents. Thomas, hearing that a customer was selling a Victorian rocking-horse, purchased it for him.

"What is his name?" asked Eric.

"Saucy," said Grandad.

Eric became Thomas's shadow and watched for Grandad's car every day. The Overland had been sold and now Thomas had an Austin 7 van, which was the workhorse of the milk round. In 1938, Thomas also bought a new Morris 8 as a family car. Emily often drove the Morris and sometimes fetched Eric to spend the day at the dairy. When she obtained her licence there were no driving tests.

Eric always remembered one special journey in the Austin van. Sadly, Jack, the Old English sheepdog, had died and Thomas and Emily had bought a pup of the same breed. Thomas took Eric to the Midland Station to collect the new Jack. This was a great thrill and Eric was bubbling with excitement as they drove down Granville Road and round to the station. The puppy had travelled all the way from Somerset and was whining for his mother. Eric was allowed to nurse him and Jack snuggled closely to Eric for comfort. There was an instant bond between them. Thomas impressed upon Eric that he must not talk to anyone about the pup riding in the van. Some milk customers might object.

"I will remember," promised Eric.

Billy had also learned to drive. His brother in law, Ernest, who worked for a motor company, had taught him. He had soon passed his test. Billy bought an Austin 7 saloon and was able to take Emmie and Eric for drives in the countryside. Unfortunately, in August 1938, the car collided with a bus. How this came about no one can be sure, but a newspaper cutting reports that '...the Austin 7 folded up like a concertina'. Somehow, Billy went under the bus and came out on the other side. Emmie's legs were badly bruised but amazingly, no one was seriously hurt. Emmie was taken into a house and seated by the fire.

"You're all of a shake!" said the kind lady, and made her a cup of tea.

While Emmie was trying to recover from her shock, the lady tried to divert Eric. "How about a ride on our rocking-horse?" she asked and led him across the room. Her good intentions were not well received. The horse was identical to Saucy but had lost its head!

"It's even knocked my horse's head off!" said the perplexed little boy. It was a relief to find his own horse unharmed when he returned home.

Billy was thankful that his wife and child were unhurt but rueful over his car. He managed to retrieve the wrecked Austin and put it in the garden. This became Eric's car and probably the best plaything he ever had.

The next major event in their lives was the birth of a daughter. On the first day of June 1939, in the middle of a heatwave, Enid was born. Emmie had always planned to call her first daughter Enid and she felt her happiness was complete. The nurse wrapped the newly born baby in a shawl and put her outside in the pram to lie in the fresh air on her first day in the big wide world. Billy lifted Eric up to see.

"Look at your new sister!" he said.

Soon after this excitement, Ernest, who had been watching out for a bargain, let Billy know of a Standard 9 car in good condition. This was duly purchased and the family was on the road again.

Emmie, recovering after Enid's birth, began to pay more attention to their home. She and Billy did some decorating, and she made new curtains. They felt very blessed in their family and their home. Billy was happy in his work and the new car was running well.

"Life," they told each other, "couldn't be better!"

34. Blackout

While Emmie and Billy were encased in their bubble of happiness, they were well aware of its fragility. War was breathing over their shoulders. Up and down the country contingency plans were being formed. In some cities during July, there had been evacuation rehearsals despite the emphasis that 'war is not inevitable'. Billy was determined that his family should be as safe as possible. They had no cellar in the house but the base of the house was set into the hillside, making deep foundations. With customary thoroughness he set about making it into a fortress. A trap-door was cut in the kitchen floor, which was strengthened. He obtained some secondhand, used railway sleepers for this purpose and also reinforced the wall adjoining their neighbours' house. When this bunker was completed he assembled a double bed down there, and Emmie kept it made up in readiness for emergencies.

The news became increasingly ominous and, like everyone else, Emmie was angered by the invasion of Poland. The plight of the Polish people affected her deeply. Their courage and their suffering haunted her. On the 3rd September 1939, Billy was at work and Emmie was at home with the children. It was no surprise when her father called – he did so frequently – but she knew at once by his serious expression that this was no ordinary visit. War had finally been declared. Billy had managed to send Thomas a message asking if he could collect Emmie and the children and take them to the dairy. Billy did not know when he would be home. He was involved with 'blacking-out' the pit.

No one knew what to expect. Would instant repercussions follow the declaration of war? Emmie was grateful for the company of her parents on that first strange day of wartime.

At the colliery, the joiners and blacksmiths were working at speed. The joiners were making huge frames for the many windows in the surface buildings. Billy, with the blacksmiths, was manufacturing large metal hinges so the frames could be opened in daylight hours. Preparations for coping with the blackout had begun the week before in Sheffield. White lines had been painted down the centre of the roads to help motorists and the pavements edged in broken white lines to help pedestrians. The windows of Deep Pits Church and the Institute were painted black.

All around the city, plans were being put into action. Air-raid sirens were tested. Men reported to units. Schools were converted to first aid centres and hospitals made ready to receive thousands of casualties. Barrage balloons appeared and emergency water tanks holding five thousand gallons were placed at vantage points.

Emmie shuddered to read of the order of hundreds of coffins, shrouds and hessian bags, but this was wartime and such matters had to be faced. She was most indignant to read that many dog and cat owners had had their pets destroyed. Eventually, identity cards were received and Emmie applied for ration books. The routine of wartime life had started. Emmie wondered about the German people. Surely they didn't want war any more than the British?

She and Billy had listened attentively to the Prime Minister's words:

'In this war we are not fighting against you – the German people – for whom we have no bitter feeling, but against a tyrannous and foresworn regime.'

Anderson shelters were delivered to the residents of Essex Road. These had to be put in place within a week of delivery otherwise they were removed and given to someone else. Billy dug the shelter in deeply and bolted the arched sections together. He built a very strong blast wall behind it and covered the shelter with a good layer of earth. Finally he obtained some large, heavy stone slabs and positioned them as a pitched roof. He was grateful for the shelter. Not everyone had them. The people of Frecheville, on the outskirts of Sheffield, complained bitterly. Some of them converted the entrance to a nearby disused coalmine.

Billy fitted the bunks into the shelter and tried to make it as comfortable and draught-free as possible. Emmie packed a case of necessities to keep in there. Changes were taking place all around, and it was hard to see families being separated as men and women joined the armed forces. Emmie's cousin, Ronnie, who had joined the army in 1938, was already driving tanks. His brother Walter, who was in the Territorial Army, had to report for duty the day after war broke out. Emmie hoped that the war would be over before their younger brothers would be called up.

1940 was a tragic year for this family. The youngest son, Gerald, aged eleven, died from a sudden illness on 28th March. Teddy, one of Emmie's closest cousins, was away with the army too. Her cousins were very important to her because she had no brothers and sisters. Emmie prayed fervently that they would all return safely.

Billy was in a reserved occupation and, like many others in the same position, felt he should be fighting for his country. His choice would have been the Navy, but as he told himself, his work was vital and he must do it as well as he could. When, on the 14th May, Anthony Eden announced the formation of the Local Defence Volunteers, Billy joined immediately. Thousands of Sheffield men volunteered and were issued with armbands. Uniforms were not available until later. This Defence Corps became the Home Guard. Billy was in the 69th Battalion.

There was a new spirit of determination at this stage. Neville Chamberlain had just resigned, a tired man. Winston Churchill took his place and told the nation, "I have nothing to offer but blood, toil, tears and sweat."

It was not easy to maintain normality amid the anxiety and the shortages, but Emmie was determined that her children should enjoy their childhood as much as possible. Emmie enjoyed it with them and filled their days with walks, songs and stories. Eric loved to go with Grandad and have dinner at the dairy. Billy's car had been parked and covered in a shed at the dairy when the war began, and soon afterwards he had regretfully sold it. An auto-cycle had replaced it. When work was over he often collected Eric from the dairy. Grandma put a cushion on the rack behind the saddle and Eric perched behind Billy for the ride home. The next time Grandad fetched Eric the cushion was returned. The cushion went to and fro with Eric.

Emmie found that there was still plenty to laugh at even in those dark days and thought some things were taken far too seriously. Women, who were now in jobs previously carried out by men, had begun to wear trousers – 'slacks', as they called them – and this was considered revolutionary. One irate reader sent a letter to the paper saying: 'Why don't the police arrest them? Should a man be seen in public masquerading as a woman, he would very quickly be hauled before the magistrates'.

Sometimes it was impossible not to dwell on the natural fears for loved ones. Emmie's cousin Walter had survived dangers in Norway and was now sailing round the coast of South Africa. He was on his way to Egypt. Emmie's anxiety for her cousin Teddy was even greater. He was in France where, under intense bombardment, Dunkirk was being evacuated. It began on Sunday 26th May. Thanks to hundreds of fishing boats, pleasure boats, and all manner of small craft adding their support to the Royal Navy, men were being rescued. Everywhere people waited for news. As each day passed they clung to their hopes that their loved ones would return. By the 2nd June the evacuation was nearly complete and there was still no news of Teddy. Emmie felt for Aunt Ada and her cousin Norah. They had lost Barbara. Were they now to lose Teddy?

On the 3rd June Emmie took Eric and Enid to see their grandparents. She wandered into the dairy and gazed through the window down City Road. As she stared into the distance, a khaki-clad figure came into sight. He drew nearer and she thought she recognised the way he walked. Her heart stood still. She was through the door in a second. It could be him! Then she was sure, and flying down the road to meet him. Tears flowed as they hugged each other.

Then Emmie, seeing the utter exhaustion in his face, said, "Come on home."

There was great rejoicing in Don Terrace that night.

335,000 men had been rescued from the beaches at Dunkirk. Sadly, 30,000 troops were killed, missing or wounded. The war was taking a terrible toll.

35. Sheffield Waits

One hot summer morning, Eric was delighted to see the rocking-horse in the garden. He ate his breakfast quickly and ran out to play. Emmie finished dressing Enid and carried her out. Eric made room for her on the saddle and held her tightly. Emmie had her camera ready and took a photo. Moments such as these had to be treasured. She wanted her children to have happy memories even under the shadow of war. Emmie thought it was a pity that children should have to grow up too quickly. Eric already had to act responsibly when danger threatened. Sometimes an aeroplane flew over and Eric pulled Enid under the kitchen table. He was well drilled in the shelter routine and Emmie was grateful for his 'man about the house' attitude when the awful wail of the sirens began. Mostly this was at night when Billy was on guard duty. She and the children saw very little of Billy. When he wasn't at work he was on guard duty. Emmie

watched the children rocking together and cherished their laughter.

"Tonight," she thought, "he will be able to see them before they go to bed."

She knew he would come home after six o'clock, eat his meal, change into uniform, kiss them all and rush up the hill to his duty at Manor Castle. The following morning he would come home for breakfast at seven, change for work, pick up his snap tin, kiss them all goodbye again and set off on his 'grey mare' – the auto cycle.

Billy and the other men on guard duty took turns to take a nap under a flat roof. A siren was fitted under the roof. When the alarm sounded the vibrations almost lifted them out of bed! During a raid, it was very noisy because the guns were close by and as the anti-aircraft batteries went into action, there was an orchestra of firing. Billy was intrigued by the rocket guns but was prevented from training to man them. Men on shift work were not included due to the strict rotas worked by the gunners.

When Billy was on guard duty, Emmie slept lightly and was out of bed in seconds when the sirens started. The children's siren suits lay open, Eric's small wellingtons threaded through the legs of his. The zips were pulled up in no time. After a quick check that all the air raid instructions had been followed, they were on their way to the shelter. One night, Emmie asked Eric to pick something up from the kitchen table. Misunderstanding, but eager to help, he picked up a tin of Golden Syrup. All the way through the garden, the treacle ran down his siren suit and into his wellingtons! Emmie was dismayed but saw the funny side of the situation. Somehow she managed to clean him and reassure the children. Nights in the shelter were long. It was not surprising that Enid's chief memory of the shelter was to be a khaki sleeve passing a khaki enamel jug through the shelter door. When Billy came home at odd hours he made a jug of hot cocoa for his family. That sleeve was a welcome sight.

*   *   *   *   *

In the wider world, the war became increasingly complex. On the 10th June, Italy declared war on France and Britain. Next day Australia, New Zealand and South Africa declared war on Italy. The Royal Air Force bombed Turin and Italian East Africa. The Italians bombed Malta. Paris prepared for a siege as the Luftwaffe struck the City. The RAF attacked German ships in Norway.

"The whole world has gone mad," thought Emmie.

While war was spreading tragedy around the globe, attacks in England were increasing. Serious bombing started in London during August and the Battle of

Britain began. Sheffield and other provincial cities sent anti-aircraft teams to help and also to observe. Their turns would come and they needed to know the worst.

In September, Eric started school at Manor Lane. He went bravely, carrying his gas mask. Emmie missed him and prayed for his safety at school. The whole family missed him. Grandad was quite lost. Billy was working longer hours at the pit. Keeping up production of coal was important. Factories needed coal for the manufacture of all the components of ships, guns, tanks, and planes. The Sheffield factories decided to carry on working normally during air-raids and only stopped if their rooftop spotters reported enemy planes. One of the problems was that if blast furnaces were stopped it took some time to start them again. Emmie's cousin, Ken, was involved in producing non-ferrous metal to be placed on the sides of ships. It was hoped that this would reduce the attraction of magnetic mines as they sailed around the coast.

The Vickers Works in Sheffield contained the only drop-hammer in the country capable of forging crankshafts for Spitfires and Hurricanes. The workers there had a punishing schedule. Like all Sheffield people, Emmie

and Billy were proud of their city with its many specialist steel works, but they knew that this made Sheffield a prime target for the Germans.

November came. On the 14th of that month, four hundred tons of bombs were dropped on Coventry. Many people were killed, injured or made homeless. The cathedral was not quite destroyed. The spire was still standing and remained a symbol of hope amid the desolation.

Before the end of November, Birmingham, Southampton, Bristol, and Liverpool had all been severely blitzed. While news of doom and gloom encircled them, Emmie had news of her own for Billy. Another baby was on the way. They gazed at each other with mixed emotions. What a time to have a baby! Billy held her close.

"A baby is God's gift," he said, "and one day this wretched war will be over."

So, even more closely bound together, they faced an uncertain future, and Sheffield waited.

36. Bombers' Moon

It was Thursday evening on the 12th December 1940. Billy, just home from work, was cheerful. Tonight he was not on guard duty and, using some ingenuity, Emmie had managed to cook something that smelled delicious. The family was soon round the table and Billy was enjoying the warmth after the bitterness of the winter night.

"This tastes good," he said.

A few seconds later, the stomach-churning sound of the sirens disturbed their peace and quiet. Immediately, the German bombers were overhead. Emmie was not just afraid. She was cross and frustrated.

"Blow Hitler!" she exclaimed. "I'm going to eat my dinner."

Billy looked at her.

"This could be a bad raid," he warned. "Where do you want to go – the cellar or the Anderson?"

Emmie regretted her temper and said, "Perhaps we should go into the shelter."

The meals were abandoned on their plates. Quick checks were made and Emmie carried Enid into the garden. The child's eyes were wide and in that instant the scene was imprinted on her mind. A bombers' moon lit the garden and the path leading to the shelter was brilliantly white with frost. Black shapes travelled above and below as the planes cast their shadows across the land. Great beams of searchlights criss-crossed the sky and rockets streaked into the air leaving blazing trails behind them. It was a breathtaking sight, almost beautiful, but deadly sinister. Billy soon had them in the shelter and made Emmie, with Enid, as comfortable as possible in one bunk. He tucked Eric beside him on the other. The night of terror had begun.

Billy listened to the planes, mentally identifying them. They were approaching over the Manor and the anti-aircraft guns kept up constant fire. He looked at Emmie's tense face lit by the candle flame, the baby miraculously asleep in her arms, and the courageous little boy at his side. The bombs began to fall – hundreds of high explosives and thousands of incendiaries. The night was a nightmare of noise. How many times did they say "I love you"? How many times did their eyes say "Goodbye"? How many prayers rose to Heaven?

Outside, a mighty landmine demolished the main building of Manor Lane School, throwing up great balls of clay. One of them hurtled through the roof of twenty-two Essex Road, and Billy and Emmie closed their eyes and held their breath as the shelter shook around them.

Wave upon wave of planes passed over. Emmie, clutching her baby with both arms, sat with her knees up to give Enid more protection. As time passed, she felt stiff and cramped.

"I should like to stretch out," she told Billy, "but I daren't."

Billy encouraged her. "Stretch out, love, just for a few minutes."

Emmie slid her feet down the bunk and pushed them against the shelter wall. At that instant there was a deafening crack above their heads and the blast stung Emmie's feet. Her whole body sang. Amazingly, they were all still alive. They heard a sliding, rattling sound against the shelter door and knew that they were trapped. Then gradually the sounds of planes, guns and bombs became less frequent. Voices could be heard and the familiar noises of shovelling began. Eventually the door was opened sufficiently for them to be pulled up into the fresh air. Their rescuers were ARPs (Air Raid Precaution Volunteers) and some of their neighbours. Emmie and Billy thanked them and looked up at their badly damaged home. They knew they were not allowed to enter it. Eric had different priorities. His Austin 7 – the one damaged in the crash – was untouched.

"Hitler didn't bomb my car!" he cried triumphantly.

Billy surveyed the shelter. A bomb had deflected from the angled stone slabs and landed elsewhere. One of the large stone slabs had split. So that was the ear-splitting crack they had heard. Those slabs had saved their lives.

They made their way to the pavement. Billy put the case down. It was packed with some necessities including identity cards, ration books and some of Emmie's precious photos. Billy was involved for some time helping neighbours. Mrs Price next door was upset because her budgie was trapped in the pantry. Billy rescued it. Their other neighbour – a rather aloof, elderly widow – walked up the road, a long blanket draped round her shoulders trailing in the road. She was clearly in shock but refused all help. She was walking to Frecheville. Billy and Emmie were glad to see Mr and Mrs Dickson alive. Their house had been badly damaged too.

Emmie sat on the case with Eric, Enid and several other frightened children around her.

"Let's play 'going to the seaside'," she said.

The game was just developing when Eric said that he could hear a ticking noise. Emmie said it must be the alarm clock in the case. Suddenly the air-raid warden rushed up and urgently told them to move. When Emmie stood up she understood his concern. They were sitting on the edge of a crater and the ticking was a live bomb!

A lorry arrived and began to fill with people forced to leave their homes. Emmie and her family were offered a ride to the Manor Top where soup was being served in the library and where they could spend the night. They declined with thanks and began to walk up Essex Road. Billy carried Enid and Emmie held Eric's hand. It was about 3 a.m. and some bombing continued. On St. Aidan's Road a woman leaned out of her bedroom window. She was half-mad with shock and rescuers were trying to persuade her to come out. They could see that the roof was on fire. Enough help was there so Emmie and Billy continued walking up City Road with their children. Reaching a gap in the houses they turned to look at Sheffield. The whole city seemed to be on fire and a frightening glow lit the sky. It was a sobering sight. They trudged along as far as Billy's old home. There they found everyone alive and settled in the shelter. Dolly was on one bunk and Ernest was in the other with Neil. Grandma lay between them in a deck chair covered in a silk eiderdown.

"Whatever are you doing out on a night like this?" demanded Dolly. "It's ridiculous!"

"We just wanted to know if all was well," said Billy. "We're going to check on Emmie's parents now."

It was not far to the dairy where Emmie felt overcome at the sight of her parents alive and well. There they received a comforting welcome. They were not the only refugees. Emily always had an open door and eighteen people had sought refuge there. They were all to stay for a while in that small, two-up-two-down house.

Next morning, when Emmie came downstairs, she observed a child's blue woollen jumper drying over the oven door. A cuddly toy dog was on the mantelpiece. Emily said, "Mr Webster sent them for you. He thought you might be glad."

Emmie thought of the home they had left behind them. Her new curtains had been blowing in rags upon the railings and the rocking-horse's head sticking incongruously through the glass panes of the front door. The blast had blown the front door inwards. At the moment they had practically nothing. The blue jumper and the toy dog were each a godsend. Her heart was full.

37. Wartime Christmas

After their ordeal in the Blitz, Emmie and Billy rested for a few hours but were too shocked to sleep properly. Eric, being resilient as most children are, was awake and ready to take the milk round with Grandad. Billy was away to work as usual. All around Sheffield, people were going about their business no matter what they had endured.

The milkman was especially welcome. Water supplies were cut-off almost everywhere and emergency supplies, with standpipes, had not reached many people yet. Everyone had a story to tell. Most of them were harrowing but others told of great courage and inspiration. News was being passed by word of mouth. The press was censored so the full extent of the damage was not revealed immediately. The tragedy at the Marples Hotel soon became common knowledge. The greatest loss of life was suffered there. When Grandad reached Manor Lane, Eric saw the devastation of his school.

When customers spoke to him he repeated, "Hitler bombed my house. Hitler bombed my school. Hitler didn't bomb my car."

Bernard Street had been badly hit. Grandad and Eric stared up at the interior of a terraced house. Only the adjoining wall still stood. A bed, apparently unharmed, was still upstairs, balanced on a few remaining floorboards. Grandad wondered if someone still lay beneath the bedclothes. As they stared the floor gave way and the bed crashed down. No one was in the bed.

At the dairy, Emmie was doing her best to help her mother to provide for her enlarged family. She and Thomas had taken in a couple with three little boys. Somehow, everyone was fed and Emmie was good at occupying the children.

On Sunday night the sirens went again. This time Billy was with the Home Guard and found himself driving an ambulance in Sheffield. At Don Terrace the

Air Raid Warden, Billy Bodsworth, who lived next door to Emily and Thomas, was keen to make sure that everything was done properly. He stood in his doorway, blew his whistle loudly, donned his tin hat, and fell over the doorstep. Everyone was ready to go to appointed shelters. A folded sheet lay on Emily's sideboard in case of gas. The sheet would be dipped in a bucket of water and hung from a line over the door if gas was suspected. The bucket of water stood ready too, and at the last moment someone kicked it over.

During the chaos, Eric said brightly, "I'm glad I'm wearing my wellies!"

At last, they were on their way up the long garden. They descended into the shelter to find it standing in water. This was another cue for Eric. "I'm glad I'm wearing my wellies!"

Everyone squeezed on to the bunks, glad to be together. The planes with their dreaded burdens returned to the already stricken city. Once again, there was an incessant cacophony of bombs and guns. Emmie could hear the gun they called the 'Big Woofer' and prayed for the men and women defending Sheffield. She thought of Billy and wondered where he was. Enid slept but Eric was awake. He was distracted by the pigs grunting in the sty behind the shelter.

Thankfully, this raid was shorter than the first Blitz but again there was a great loss of life and terrible destruction. The enemy did not achieve the demolition of Sheffield's industry, the main purpose of the raid. Flares set on the moors had misled them. Sadly, this deception resulted in the deaths and injuries of many ordinary people and made thousands homeless. The people paid the price.

Blitz-connected traffic came and went along City Road. The families who lived there watched with interest. A few days after the second Blitz, Emmie took Eric and Enid to stand on the pavement. A convoy of four fire engines was returning to Woodhouse from Sheffield. The men looked tired and dirty as well they might. They had been in the city from the beginning of the first Blitz. Now they were on their way home. They grinned and waved to the groups of people who gathered to cheer them on their way.

Just as Emmie began to think that the worst was over she became anxious about Enid. The cold she had caught was rapidly turning into something worse. The family doctor came as soon as he was called. Dr. Downie, a quiet Scot, had delivered Enid, and Emmie trusted him.

"It's pneumonia," he said seriously. "Try to keep her temperature down and call me if her condition deteriorates. I'll come again in the morning."

Emmie and Billy were very alarmed and for a few days it was touch and go. Eventually a turning point was reached and Emmie's baby smiled again. Emmie smiled too and everyone in this crowded household breathed a sigh of relief.

There was a glimmer of hope on the war front too. General Wavell's forces pushed the Italians back in the Western Desert. Thirty thousand Italian troops had been captured. Cousin Walter had been part of this force. Emmie hoped they would have good news of him.

It was not an easy time for anyone but every day someone in Don Terrace would say, "How lucky we are to be alive!" No one could ask for more, but Christmas was close and the adults pondered over the problem of presents for the children. Gifts had been bought for the three brothers but they had been stored in a blitzed newsagents. Presents for Eric and Enid were upstairs at Essex Road. The house was being guarded by soldiers in case of time-bombs, but Billy was allowed in for a few minutes after dark one night. Emmie kept a pile of picture books for Sunday school prizes stored in boxes and they were all safe and clean! Each child came down on Christmas morning to find that the Blitz had not prevented Father Christmas from keeping his promise. He had been.

Thomas and Emily were happy to see the two young families enjoying their Christmas Day. Everyone agreed that yes, of course, "Grandma has done us proud for Christmas dinner." (She knew how to make a tin of salmon go a long way.) How thankfully they said their grace. Afterwards, they listened to the King's speech. When 'God Save The King' was played they all stood to attention. All over the country an army of ordinary people stood to attention. The Blitz had done its worst, but it had not broken their spirit.

38. 'Another One Alive!'

It was a family joke that Billy could sleep on a clothes-line. Actually, this was a useful skill because he had little opportunity to sleep in his bed. He worked long hours at the pit and never missed Home Guard duty. If there was an air-raid he walked to Essex Road – a mile away – to take his turn at fire-watching. If the 'All Clear!' sounded, he returned to the dairy. Sometimes he would be almost back to the dairy when the sirens began to wail again. Wearily he would return to Essex Road. Occasionally he snatched a nap on the living room floor of a neighbour's house. Mr and Mrs Dickson had been able to return to their home six weeks after the Blitz. Emmie and Billy were to wait a long time for their seriously damaged house to be repaired. Billy could always find a haven at the Dicksons' home.

The Blitz had caused damage at Woodburn Road Colliery too. The pit headgear stood on a massive wooden frame and a bomb had blown a section of one of the main supports away. This was a mighty wooden 'leg' measuring about fifteen feet long by fourteen inches square. Billy designed and made enormous metal clamps in the blacksmith's shop. No good wood was available to replace the leg so he organised the hoisting of an old telegraph pole up to the headgear. This was successfully clamped into place, and the big wheel turned again.

Emmie was busy too. When the children were occupied she helped in the dairy. Milk was now delivered in bottles so bottle-washing was a daily activity. Eric had great fun using the machine which fitted cardboard caps on to the filled bottles.

Everywhere attempts were being made to carry on normally. The ruined stores in Sheffield found new premises as quickly as possible. Cockaynes set up in the grill-room of the Grand Hotel. Walsh's moved to The Mount at Broomhill. Marks and Spencer re-opened at the old Lansdowne Cinema. British Home Stores moved to Norfolk Street. Brightside and Carbrook Co-op found a new home in the Playhouse.

The re-opening of schools varied. Apart from finding premises, there was a great shortage of teachers. Many teachers had been called up into the forces. The infants' department at Manor Lane was not fit to be used and the junior department was a ruin. Some of the children, including Eric, were transferred to Prince Edward's at the Manor Top. Eric, who had only just started school before the Blitz, was apprehensive. Emmie had mixed emotions too, but knew she must encourage him to be independent.

Eric was astonished and jubilant to find his teacher from Manor Lane there to greet him. Miss Brunt's face lit up when she saw him and she threw her arms around him. Tears ran down her face.

"Another one alive!" she cried. "Thank God!" Eric was equally happy to see Miss Brunt, and Emmie left him in her care with a much lighter heart.

Emmie could now feel the movement of the baby she was carrying and began to plan for its arrival. "Do you think there is any chance I could have my pram?" she asked Billy.

"I'll do my best," promised Billy. He still needed permission to enter his own house. This was granted and he made his way in carefully. The rocking-horse still stood by the front door. He gave it an affectionate pat and noticed that the plywood panel of the kitchen door had disappeared. The blast had thrown up all the floorboards but his railway sleepers were still in place. It was dark. Strangely, the table was still standing. Billy thought of the times his children had sheltered beneath it. Whatever was on the table? Closer inspection showed that the tall, chimney-like shapes were fungus growing on their abandoned dinners! He noticed that the wrecked roof above him was well covered and was glad. Where was the pram?

He found it blown against the pantry door and pulled at it. Why was it so heavy? He scrambled over a heap of rubble and realised the pram was packed with clay. It was no easy task to manoeuvre it outside where he began to dig out the clay. When the pram was lighter to push, he set off for the dairy with his prize. He knew Emmie would be delighted whatever its condition. She rushed out to kiss him and greeted her pram like an old friend.

"Poor old pram!" she cried.

Emmie and her mother both worked hard to clean the pram and were not satisfied until it was spotless. Even then, Emmie thought the clay left a slight lingering odour. Billy attended to the springs and the wheels. The centre section of the base lifted out and Enid was able to sit with her feet in the well and play with her books and toys. She enjoyed this elevated position for short spells but, like any active toddler, preferred playing with the dog or pushing Emmie's old bear on wheels around the yard. Watching her play, Emily remembered Emmie at the same stage. She was happy to have her grandchildren with them, to see them and to know that they were safe.

"Soon," Emily thought, "there will be an addition to the family." She hoped that the baby about to be born under their roof would be delivered safely.

Nothing as savage as the Blitz had taken place in 1941 but most weeks air-raid warnings still sounded. There was a newly mounting toll of dead and injured. More than four hundred people had been made homeless when bombs and landmines were dropped on Wadsley and Southy Hill districts.

Emmie realised that the baby was coming on the 21st June. All was ready and the midwife arrived. During the night the sirens sounded and planes were heard overhead. In no little discomfort Emmie crawled under a table for protection. As the night wore on this was repeated several times.

Dawn came and Emmie lay in bed listening to snatches of news from across the stairs. Her mind was clouded by her condition but the frequency of the word 'invasion' filled her with fear. Was this long and frightening night the beginnings of a German invasion? Billy put her mind at rest. It was indeed a German invasion but, fortunately for Britain, the Germans had invaded Russia. It was at this turning point of the war that Emmie gave birth to a little girl. Her delighted parents called her Christine.

Even in the midst of war, the miracle of new life was transforming. Emmie watched Billy nursing their new daughter and forgot her pain and fear. Eric and Enid gazed in fascination and counted fingers and toes. Thomas and Emily smiled in joy and relief.

Visitors came frequently to see Emmie and her new baby during her 'lying-in' period. Billy's sister Dolly called. She inspected the new arrival whom she saw as a ready-made sister for Neil.

"You already have a boy and a girl," she told Emmie. "Now there's another mouth to feed."

Emmie was shocked to think that anyone could consider taking her baby away from her, and held Christine even closer. "I'm sorry, Dolly," she said. "I really can't part with her."

Later, when Billy came in, Emmie told him. Billy's arm went round her and he laughed. "You should know better than to take notice of our Doll," he said.

Her next visitor was Aunt Florrie, the odd, unschooled sister of Emily. She was rather rough-and-ready but Emmie had loved her since she was small. She could talk to Aunt Florrie.

"Do you think we have been very wrong to have a baby in wartime?"

"Nay, lass, tha's browt sum joy into the world when there's not much to laugh at. When such terrible things are going on around us, a new baby gives us all a bit of 'ope." She paused and her chubby features squeezed into a smile. "Sithee, she's a real pretty baby."

Aunt Florrie's words comforted Emmie, but a few weeks later there was heart-stopping anxiety. Eric and Enid contracted whooping cough. Christine was isolated in the attic and Emmie fed and changed her there. Eric and Enid were dangerously ill. It was quite common for children to die from whooping cough. They whooped and vomited constantly. Doctor Downie came twice daily to see them and refused all payment. Emmie and Billy were never to forget this kindness. Maybe the good doctor felt there was little he could do. There were no antibiotics then. He agreed that isolating Christine was sensible and reassured Emmie.

"While you are breast-feeding, your baby will be immune to most things."

Christine certainly was a model baby who fed and slept by turns. Thomas joked that this was due to the hops in the cows' fodder. Emmie was drinking extra milk straight from the cows.

Day after day, Emmie and Billy watched their children growing weaker. Night after night, they nursed them in their feverish restlessness. One afternoon, Eric began to whoop convulsively and Emmie ran to him, instinctively pulling him upright. He had broken a blood vessel and Emmie thought he was dying. Thomas rushed for Doctor Downie but by the time he came back with the Doctor, Eric was calmer. The bleeding had stopped and Emmie was holding him against her. She told the doctor what had happened.

"You did the right thing to lift him into a sitting position," he said. "That probably saved his life."

After this incident, Emmie dared not leave the children alone for a second. But this had been the worst moment. Gradually the children began to cough less. They 'slept themselves better' and Emily tried to tempt them with small tastes of nourishing food. Eric and Enid were not the only children to succumb to illness. Damp shelters on cold nights were not conducive to good health and food shortages did not help. Once again, Emmie thanked God that her children had survived.

War continued to rage around the world but life at the dairy became more settled.

*　　*　　*　　*　　*

In November Emmie was thrilled to see Teddy again. He was home on leave to be married. Emmie liked his attractive, fashionable wife. Elsie had a bubbly personality and a warm, generous nature. Teddy looked smart in his uniform and Elsie so beautiful. They had only a short time together. How cruel it seemed that war should part them so soon.

December came, and the Japanese attacked Pearl Harbour. The following day Great Britain and America declared war on Japan. Christmas was coming and everyone thought of those they loved who were far away from home, especially those overseas. Walter was still in Africa and his brother was there too. Ronnie had joined the army in 1938 and was driving tanks in Libya. Emmie longed for her cousins to return safely. Christmas was quiet.

The following weeks were full of anxiety for Emmie. On New Year's Day, Eric was ill with gastric flu and severe nosebleeds. He recovered from the flu but the nosebleeds became more frequent. He was very white and Doctor Downie told Emmie his nose would have to be cauterised. This was done at the Royal Hospital and Emmie was very proud when the doctor told her he had been splendid.

"He never made a murmur," she said to Billy.

It was Billy's turn next for hospital treatment. After an accident at work, a piece of steel was removed from his hand. He came home stitched and bandaged.

Worse was to come. Eric caught diphtheria. Emmie and all the family watched as he was wrapped in a red blanket and taken by ambulance to Lodge Moor Hospital. That night the sirens went again, and Emmie and Billy thought of their little boy who lay on a flat bed in a white hospital gown. Emmie wrote in her diary: 'He was a brave little chap. He never cried. His hospital number is 1410.' It was several days before Emmie and Billy were allowed to see Eric. He was still dangerously ill but smiled when he saw the little gold aeroplane Billy had made for him.

Throughout the seven long weeks he lay in hospital, prayers were said for him at Deep Pits Chapel. All the customers on the milk round knew the chatty little boy who accompanied his grandad on Saturday mornings and asked after him daily. Thomas could only shake his head for a while but eventually Eric turned the corner and Thomas was cheerful again. Eric sat up in bed and played with his spinning tops. Thomas had made these simple toys from cardboard milk tops with sharpened matches through their centres. Thomas had made enough to supply all the children in the ward.

At last Eric came home. He was painfully thin and hardly able to stand. Emmie wrote in her diary: "Eric can't walk this morning but it's grand to have him home."

When Eric was well again, Emmie managed to have a photograph taken of her three children together. Eric was wearing a Naval Officer's suit Emmie had obtained second-hand. It was taken at Cole Brothers. The photographer was very patient. Christine wanted to run about and Eric had to hold on to her feet. Emmie was very thrilled with her picture.

Spring came and repairs began on the house at Essex Road. Eventually the family prepared to return. The day came when the big pram was pushed down the passage with Enid and Christine sitting one at each end. Emmie, Billy and Eric stood on the pavement in some excitement. Everyone felt strange. Thomas and Emily had sheltered and cared for them for eighteen months. Emmie kissed her parents and thanked them, as she had done many times already, for all they had done. Her mother's eyes filled with tears and she couldn't speak as they waved goodbye. She and Thomas watched them out of sight and went back into the quiet house.

"Life must go on," Emily told herself firmly. She filled the kettle and switched on the radio. Vera Lynn's voice floated out:

> *There'll be bluebirds over*
> *The white cliffs of Dover*

Emily put a loaf on the table. Her mind was not on Vera Lynn. Then she heard:

> *The shepherd will tend his sheep*
> *The valley will bloom again*
> *And Jimmy will go to sleep*
> *In his own little room again.*

She turned to Thomas and wept.

39. Back to the Dairy

"Secondary boys should wear shorts to save cloth up to the age of seventeen," said a letter to the paper. It continued, "Generally speaking, northern boys are more sturdily built than those in the south and look their best in shorts." Everyone had ideas on how to economise in the support of the nation and Emmie, along with most mothers, did her best. Her children were encouraged to be proud of 'hand-me-downs' and expected not to grumble about darns in their socks. She was adept at repairing Wellingtons. She stuck on soles made out of old hot water bottles and put patches on the upper parts made from bicycle repair kits. Jumble sales were a real opportunity and she appreciated the efforts of the Women's Voluntary Service. Clothes taken in to the W.V.S. were exchanged for points. The points could be given in return for something outgrown by someone else. Emmie took a pride in making sure her children were properly clad even if it was a case of 'make-do-and-mend'.

There was a shortage of nearly everything. The 'Dig for Victory' slogan prompted people into planting vegetables on shelter rooftops, railway embankments and grass verges. Other food was rationed and shared carefully. Emmie was delighted to find that honey, which was not rationed, could sometimes be obtained from Mrs Dickson. Edna, their daughter, was in the Land Army. She was very happy on the farm where she was based, and encouraged to keep bees. She was able to send honey home. The children liked visiting Mrs Dickson. She was kind with rosy cheeks and a big smile. The house seemed to smell of honey.

While Eric was at school Emmie sometimes walked into Sheffield, with Enid on reins and Christine in a rather primitive pushchair. There they called at the 'puppy market'. It was a dark place with great, shabby wooden doors and a lumpy earth floor. Rabbits in stacked hutches lined the walls and there were boxes of adorable puppies and kittens. Emmie sighed over them but she was there to buy day-old chicks. Enid carefully nursed a box containing a dozen chicks on the homeward journey in the tram. Livestock was not allowed on the trams and Emmie hoped the 'peep! peep!' sounds would go unnoticed by the conductor. At home, the chicks ran around for a few days in the kitchen pecking at the tufty bits of the repaired rag rugs. When the children came down in the mornings they sat very still in their nightclothes, amused by the chicks pecking their toes. After a few days, the chicks were put in a coop in the garden. Emmie usually managed to rear some and when they began to lay she was thrilled. A triumphant cackle from the garden resulted in excited children trying to find the egg.

Many things were being collected for war purposes. Bins were placed at certain points for the collection of bones. The bones were made into glue. Emmie was a little sad to see the pretty iron railings removed from their low front wall. She knew that more important things had been taken. Two historic cannons had been lifted from the Crimean War Memorial in Sheffield as part of a great gathering of scrap iron. Emmie told herself it was wrong to even wish that life was different. When unspeakable horrors were happening in so many parts of the world, what did a few railings matter?

Emmie took Christine to the clinic for a routine visit and found that her own sleeve was being rolled up. Before she had time to question it, she had received a typhoid injection. A German invasion was still considered a possibility and with it the poisoning of water supplies. Selected mothers were being protected so that they would be in a position to take charge in such a crisis.

Autumn came, and in Egypt, the German and Italian forces were defeated. News came that cousin Walter was safe. In celebration of this victory, Churchill ordered that church bells could be rung in November. On 15th November, Emmie rejoiced to hear bells ringing out across Sheffield. The bells of Fulwood Church played 'Fight the Good Fight'. In Derbyshire, the bells of Derwent Parish Church rang for the last time. The village was cleared at the end of the month for the building of Derwent reservoir.

Emmie and Billy began to prepare for Christmas. Simple, home-made presents and some picture books had been hidden away. Christmas Day was always spent at Grandma Richardson's with a brief visit to see Grandad and Grandma Evans at the dairy. Eric talked about preparations at school and this year Enid understood about Father Christmas. Christine didn't understand but joined in the general excitement. Emmie told them Christmas stories. She wanted them to understand the real meaning of Christmas.

Then disaster struck! Early one morning Thomas and Emily were returning from fetching milk. The roads were very icy, and as they descended the steep hill into Gleadless, their van slid across the road into the path of a petrol tanker. They were both thrown into the road. An ambulance took them to hospital. A stranger brought Emmie the news and the neighbours rallied to help. Emmie ran to catch a tram. The couple sitting behind her were discussing the accident.

"They've covered the woman up for dead," one said. Emmie dared not ask what else they knew. At the hospital she found her father able to speak but in great pain. To her relief, her mother was not dead but unconscious. Her head had hit the mirror and she was black-and-blue. Later Billy joined her at the hospital. Together they reassured Thomas that Emily was alive, but did not tell him of their fear that she would not regain consciousness. Thomas worried about the milk round.

"Stop worrying," said Emmie. "We'll stay at the dairy."

So once again, the family left their home and returned to the dairy. Thomas had employed two sisters to help with the work. They lived in as Emmie's friend Evelyn had done before she was married. Emmie took over and they managed to continue delivering milk with the help of friends. Gradually Thomas seemed to be recovering but Emily still lay unconscious.

On Christmas Eve, one of Emmie's cadets, Marie Hault, was on leave from the Wrens. A friend persuaded her to go carolling with a group around the hospitals. She was dismayed to see Tommy Evans in bed there and stayed for a few minutes to chat to him. As she joined the others in singing 'Silent Night' they entered the women's ward. The ward was candlelit for the occasion and most of the patients were sitting up in bed expectantly. The sweetness of the singing brought a sense of peace, and the young faces glowing in the candlelight brought the real Christmas message. Marie looked along the line of beds and recognised Emily lying, eyes closed, on her pillow. The carol came to an end and she asked if they could sing one around the bed of her sick friend.

Emily had been emerging from her deeply unconscious state into a strange world of dreams. The nurses had seen her move and had called her name, but she had not responded. Now, with 'Away in a Manger' echoing around her, she opened her eyes and smiled.

Marie took hold of her hand and said, "Hello, Mrs Evans." Emily nodded and closed her eyes again.

Before going home, Marie called at the dairy with her good news.

"That's the best Christmas present we could have!" Emmie said joyfully.

On Christmas Day, Emmie and Billy visited hospital to find her mother propped up against her pillows. She was back in the land of the living.

40. End of an Era

1943 brought many positive advances towards victory. Battles overseas were won, but not – of course – without loss of life. Casualties in Britain continued too, and Emmie cried when she read of the daylight bombing of a school in London in which forty-four children and their teacher were killed. The call-up age for single girls was lowered to nineteen and men were taken from reserved occupations to serve abroad. This, in turn, created more pressure on vital industries and those who worked in them.

One day, while Emmie was still helping out at the dairy, her Uncle Walter called to see Thomas and Emily. They were still recovering from their accident. Walter told them that all his children were now in the services.

"Annie tries not to show it," he told them, "but sometimes she's out of her mind with worry." He continued, "We haven't heard from Walter and Ronnie for a while. Dougie has now been called up and thinks he will be sent to Egypt. Kenny has been taken from the steelworks to join the Home Guard because they are short of men. His turn to go and fight will come. Thank goodness our young Eileen is still in this country in the Land Army."

Emmie thought of her cousins, the four little boys she had bathed in the copper when they were small and the little girl who had been her bridesmaid. How could she comfort Walter and Annie?

"They are all a credit to you, Uncle Walter," she said.

"Yes," replied Walter rather gruffly as he turned to go. "We are proud of them."

He lifted his chin and winked at his sister. "Keep on getting better." He raised the sneck and closed the door behind him.

When Thomas and Emily felt well enough to take over again, Emmie and Billy went back to Essex Road. Emmie was able to give her children more attention and she was concerned about Enid. The child did not eat well and seemed chesty. She was much more shy than her sister and brother. Emmie took her to Doctor Downie. He always remembered Enid's age because on the night that he had brought her into the world, his wife had given birth to a baby at home. He sounded Enid's chest and announced that an appointment at the hospital was necessary. There, Emmie was informed that the problem was asthma. No medication was given but the doctor insisted that rest was important. He looked at the little girl standing in front of him clad only in vest and knickers.

"She needs a woollen vest," he recommended. He smiled at Enid. "What nasty chilblains! Take her to see the doctor across the corridor and see if he can help."

The nurse showed them into another room and explained their presence. "She needs lots of exercise to stimulate her circulation," said this doctor. "Buy her a skipping rope."

"So now what do we do?" asked Emmie of Billy in exasperation.

"Take her to dancing lessons," said Billy. "You always wanted to dance. If the exercise is too much for her, we'll soon find out."

So Enid was taken to the Joan Whittaker School of Dance on Granville Road. She lined up at the barre with the other children and did her best to copy them. When it was tap dancing they took turns to hop or shuffle and rested in between. Ballet, for the younger children, was slower. Then they did stretching exercises, throwing their arms behind them and lifting their chests while Miss Whittaker called loudly and repeatedly, "Now open your lungs and open your lungs!"

Emmie, watching, thought this must be an ideal exercise for asthma. Enid loved it. Not only did it cure her asthma, it helped her to conquer her shyness. She didn't particularly like the woollen 'moon' vest that tied at the neck and had sleeves to her elbows.

Around this time Billy changed his job. He had to obtain permission from the Ministry to do this. He moved to Rotherham Main Colliery because this was the nearest pit using lock-winding ropes. He wanted to keep up with the new technology. Woodburn Road Nunnery was still using standard ropes. Lock-winding ropes were 'capped', and 'capping' was a very skilled process. Every six months, the ropes were changed and capped again to ensure absolute safety. The ends of the rope in their magnet-shaped caps stood five feet tall and metal rings were hammered down over them. Two men worked together to hammer them into place. Billy was in charge of this process. Eric was very interested and wanted to know all about it. Billy drew pictures of the men with their hammers.

"When they do this," he explained, "it's called 'ringing them down'. It makes a great noise. The men have to strike perfectly in time with each other or the job will not be done properly."

Eric was fascinated. He understood about working 'perfectly in time' because Emmie was teaching him to play the piano. He had reached 'The Bluebells of Scotland' and was beginning to think that that was enough. Hammering was much more interesting.

Occasionally there were signs that better times lay ahead. From the outbreak of war, church bells were only to be rung in case of enemy invasion but circumstances had changed. From April 1943, bells could again be rung for services. Hearing bells on Sundays lifted hearts and spirits.

The summer holidays came. Eric spent much of his time with Grandad Evans or at Flint's farm which was close by. Enid began to explore further. The house at the bottom of the garden, lower down the hillside, was the last one to be built before the war began. Next to it was an old section of field. Enid squeezed through a small gap and found herself in a paradise of gold and green. Surrounded by overgrown hawthorn and high grass, a million dandelions shone in the sunshine. She began to pick a fat bunch and their milky juice stained her fingers and her dress. The scent of their hot petals sank deeply into her memory. That scent would always bring back a vision of that magical place and the mystical solitude. She carried her bouquet back to Emmie with pride, and watched the golden flowers being arranged in a large jam jar with clear water running round their stems. The sun shone through them. Emmie told her that they were wonderful, but suggested that if she wanted to go there again to ask first and mummy would take her. Emmie was pleased that Enid shared her love for flowers. She taught her children the names of the flowers they found on their walks. The children were growing quickly.

The war dragged on. Emmie's cousin, Jack, had been released from the steelworks to join the army and had been sent to Egypt. Jack was a home-loving lad and left a wife and two children behind him. Emmie knew he would find it hard.

Eric went back to school for the autumn term. Christmas came and went. Spring changed to summer and there was more news of Emmie's cousins. Walter, who had been in India, was now on his way to Burma. Ronnie was going to Italy.

173

Dougie was still in Egypt. Emmie knew there must be more fierce fighting if the war was to be won, and prayed for her cousins.

In May, the Allied Forces finally captured Monte Cassino in Italy. Bitter and ferocious battles had continued for more than five and a half months, through freezing winter weather and almost unendurable conditions. Americans, British, Indians and French had died in their thousands on the surrounding hills. On the 18th May, New Zealanders made great advances. General Alexander brought reinforcements from the Eighth Army. On the same day a gallant Polish detachment rushed to occupy Monastery Hill. It was during these final days that Ronnie was badly injured.

It was a terrible battle with great losses. Ronnie was badly injured in an explosion there but brought back to England alive to spend six months in hospital. Ronnie had been driving a tank. He was the only survivor and the men with him were lost. Ronnie was thought to be dead but, thankfully, someone saw him move. He was in a coma for some time. The whole family was shaken but grateful for his return.

The following month, the careful plans for D-Day were put into action. On the 6th June the Allies landed in Normandy for the first 'wave' of horrendous warfare. A few days later, a second wave followed and it was at Caen that Dougie, like his brother, was badly injured in an explosion. As Walter and Annie were coping with this situation, their son Ken was transferred from the Home Guard to the army. Annie was brave but aware of the pain her boys were suffering. She was nursing in Sheffield and witnessed the shock and pain of many injured men. Sheffield hospitals had been prepared since Christmas to receive three hundred wounded men at short notice, and now they were being crowded into wards.

Emmie, troubled by this news, was also distressed because her father was seriously ill. Thomas, who had undergone an operation for cancer during the previous year, was told that the cancer had returned. He knew that it was terminal. He was sent home from hospital to a downstairs bed. Emmie took the children to see him. He wanted his granddaughters to dance for him and they performed a song and dance on the carpet. It made him smile.

"I should like a photo of my grandchildren," he said. Emmie took the children to Sheffield. She knew it would not be easy to obtain a photo in wartime. They went from photographer to photographer but each one said, "Sorry – no film." Film was being reserved for photography in planes reconnoitring over enemy territory.

That night Emmie told Billy, "My little threesome were tired but very good. They wanted a photo for Grandad because he is so poorly. I was sad and tired and then I remembered a shop down the Moor so back we trekked. The gentleman said 'Sorry – no film.' I was near to tears. I explained and – here's the result!"

The photograph was lovely. Emmie, Eric, Enid and Christine were all smiling. Their efforts had been worthwhile. Grandad loved it. His eyes hardly left it. After Emmie and the children gave it to him, he asked Eric to learn the twenty-third psalm. A week later Eric recited it solemnly. Grandad was satisfied. He gave Eric his own treasured Bible.

The next day, Thomas died. Emily and Emmie were devastated. Everyone grieved, but to Eric it seemed like the end of the world. Certainly it was the end of an era.

41. New Starts

Everyone missed Thomas. They all had their own memories of him. Memories for Enid and Christine became vague, but they had a lasting image of him wearing three pairs of spectacles on his head while he searched for another. They remembered his Windsor chair with the newspapers stuffed under the cushion. How he regularly and absentmindedly almost sat on the cat! All memories accompanied by a warm feeling of love and laughter.

Emily had everlasting and deeply personal memories of her husband, but her grief was private and she faced the future firmly. It was part of her Christian philosophy always to have hope. She joined her sister Ada in her war work – the manufacture of components for Morse code machines. The milk round was sold and the work in the busy dairy ceased. The workshop was silent. The scent of leather lingered and the old place was full of memories.

Thomas had wanted Billy to have his Morris 8 and left it to him in his will. Billy was very touched by this gesture. At first the car could only be driven sparingly because fuel was in short supply. Their first drive was to Gleadless to visit Emily's sister, Ethel. Ethel was married to Jack Haigh and they had no children. Their only child had died at birth. They loved children and were very fond of Jack's two nieces to whom they were almost second parents. They were delighted to see Emmie and her family. Emmie admired the photo of their niece, Bessie, in her Wrens' uniform. Emmie had told her children that Uncle Jack had been in the Royal Horse Guards and used to march up and down in front of Buckingham Palace. They were most impressed by this but Uncle Jack was a modest man, quiet and gentle. He took them up his well-kept garden and showed them the peas hanging in their pods, and encouraged them to pick some and eat them straight away. Eric and Christine ran off to explore, but Enid stayed, popping open the pods and enjoying her solitude.

With the sun warming her head, Enid stood between the tall, sweet-smelling peas and the tall wheat on the edge of the field. She felt very small and secure in her hiding place and was sad when her mother's voice called, "Enid! Where are you? We're going now."

While Emmie was occupied with the urgent problems following her father's death, another wartime crisis arose. Flying bombs and rocket bombs attacked the South of England, mainly targeting London. These caused terror, death and destruction. About seven thousand evacuees came to Sheffield to avoid the horrors of the V1s and V2s. Emmie was proud of the way that Sheffield responded and wished she could do more to help.

As well as trying to provide for evacuees, efforts were being made to cheer the many shocked and wounded soldiers. Miss Whittaker's dancing school was asked to put on a show in a hospital ward. Christine was dancing now, having made a spontaneous and unplanned debut at a concert at Deep Pits Chapel. A row of little girls, including Enid, had been lined up for their entrance. They all wore dresses made from old net curtains dipped in blue 'dolly-dye'. To satisfy Christine, Emmie had made a dress for her too. She was two years old and supposed to be in the

audience. Somehow she managed to join on the end of the line and appeared on stage. She copied all the actions and, rather unfairly, stole the show!

On the day of the concert, Emmie packed all the costumes into an old suitcase. Much ingenuity had gone into their creation. Butterfly wings had been made from discarded parachute silk, and the carefully ironed frills on the ballet knickers were made of bandages. Emmie also put in two small dressing-gowns with woollen cardigans stitched inside. She wanted her girls to be warm as they waited in skimpy costumes.

It was strange, dancing in a darkened ward. Beds had been pushed together and men in plaster and bandages sat in wheelchairs. Emmie looked at their worn faces. After all they had witnessed and suffered, how trite the songs and dances of little children must seem! But the men smiled and applauded. Emmie hoped it distracted them from darker thoughts.

*   *   *   *   *

Around this time Emily bought an old caravan. It was situated near Blackpool. Billy, Emmie, the children, and their beloved Grandma Evans squeezed into the Morris 8 and went for a short holiday. It was the first of many. Arriving home again, Enid dissolved into tears. What was the matter? Monkey, her old glove puppet which she had taken to the caravan, was missing! Grandad Evans had given her this himself so Monkey was doubly precious. She was inconsolable. Fortunately, a telephone had been recently installed at Essex Road, a necessity for emergency calls from Billy's work. Emmie was able to telephone the site owner who discovered Monkey lying in the rain outside the caravan. This kind lady dried him and posted him to Sheffield. Enid couldn't wait to release him from the parcel and clung to him thankfully. He looked none the worse for his adventure.

*   *   *   *   *

In August, the Allied forces were gradually bringing freedom to France. On the 25th August, Paris was liberated. Radios were switched on all over England as people listened intently to the news. Great crowds thronged the Paris boulevards to welcome General Leclerc leading the French army and the American forces.

The German garrison had hurriedly capitulated and the main enemy forces were streaming back across the Seine. Paris was French again! American, Canadian, and British troops were all on the march.

The British troops covered two hundred and six miles to Brussels from Vernon in six days. There was great pride in England when they heard of Montgomery's men entering the capital of Belgium. Flags draped the buildings and thousands of voices sang 'Tipperary' and other World War I songs.

Emmie and Billy felt the end of the war must be in sight.

By September, the evacuees began to return to London although there was still danger. The schools opened, and Enid went to school for the first time. She was able to begin at Manor Lane Infants, but the junior department was still in ruins. A neighbour of Emmie's entered this ruin out of curiosity. She stepped over the rubble into the remains of a classroom and noticed a piece of paper still clinging to a wall.

"It had your name on!" she told Emmie. Emmie looked at her in disbelief. Amazingly, it was a composition Emmie had written when she was at school entitled 'My Ideal Home'. Work was rarely put on the walls in those days but the teacher had liked it. No one had ever taken it down and it had survived the bomb!

Enid found school awesome and spent most of her days in her own little world. Each morning, Emmie gave all her children a spoon of cod-liver oil before checking that they had all they needed. She made sure Enid had her chalk rag and her hanky. A milk halfpenny was pressed into her hand with the instruction to give it 'straight to the teacher'. She hoped Enid would be all right.

Every day the teacher said, "Hold up your hanky in one hand and your chalk rag in the other". Every day the child behind Enid snatched her chalk rag. These small problems apart, Enid settled into school. She loved her teacher, Mrs Lynham. Blackboards ran round the walls of the classroom and Mrs Lynham drew pictures of Peter Rabbit in coloured chalks, telling the story.

May Day was celebrated at Manor Lane School and Emmie joined all the other proud parents to hear the children singing. Another treasured photograph was added to her collection. Enid, in her paper frock, stands at the end of the row, her headdress askew. During the dark days of war, diversions like these were welcome highlights. Emmie admired the ingenuity the teachers had used in dressing the children and the efforts they had made.

There was another new start for Billy, too. He was now at Handsworth Colliery in charge of the Furnace Drift and High Hazels Coal Preparation Plant. He was responsible for anything mechanical such as coal cutters, haulages, pumps, ventilator fans and conveyors. This increased his workload tremendously but his wartime duties were about to end. In November, the Home Guard was stood down but kept in reserve. To mark the stand-down, about eight thousand men from Barnsley, Rotherham and Doncaster marched through Sheffield. It was reported that '…for nearly an hour, men of the most remarkable civilian army ever known, marched past and saluted their commanders'. Billy, who had been in the Home Guard since the first day of its formation, was needed at the pit. He greatly regretted that he could not be there on such a momentous occasion.

When Christmas came in 1944, there may not have been illuminations, but the sight of Sheffield Town Hall clock, lit up for the first time since war began, was a glorious and welcome sight indeed!

42. Victory!

By March 1945, Germany itself was under attack. British and American forces approached from the west and the Red Army from the east. At the end of April, German forces surrendered unconditionally to General Alexander. Hitler and his wife committed suicide. On the 4th May, the German forces in North Western Germany surrendered to Montgomery. An unconditional surrender was signed at 2.41 a.m. on the 7th May at Eisenhower's headquarters. Winston Churchill announced 'Victory' to the House of Commons on the following day. The war in Europe was over and the mood across Britain was one of jubilation. Emmie and Billy, with their children, joined in the rapturous rejoicing. A large bonfire was built in the garden at Essex Road, and Eric allowed the deteriorating remains of his Austin Seven to be placed on the top. Emmie tied red, white and blue ribbons in Enid and Christine's hair. Family, friends, and neighbours came to the party.

It was evening when the bonfire was lit. Street parties had been held all day and continued late into the night. People danced, Union Jacks flew bravely, and bands played. Emmie and Billy, with the happy crowd on Essex Road, looked out across Sheffield where hundreds of bonfires were triumphantly blazing. Much later that night, Emmie and Billy watched the fires glowing around Sheffield and felt a sense of peace.

"I wish Dad had lived long enough to see this day," Emmie sighed.

"Never mind," comforted Billy. "He knew the worst was over."

Victory had been won in Europe, but in the Far East fierce fighting continued and was only brought to an end by the devastation of two atomic bombs. Japanese surrender came on the 2nd September. Rejoicing this time was tempered by the sombre contemplation of the dreadful means used to achieve peace.

SMAILIA
EGYPT
1942

As the weeks passed, people everywhere began trying to mend their broken lives. Emmie thanked God that so many of those she loved had survived. Some of them were still overseas.

Her young cousin Ken had only been sent abroad recently, first to India and then to Haifa in Palestine. Her cousin Jack was at Ishmael in Egypt. He was a lance corporal in a quartermaster's stores. A sergeant major's training had been offered to him but all Jack wanted was to be demobbed and to return to his family. Cousin Teddy had arrived home safely. Cousin Walter would be coming home soon. He had been in action throughout the war and was awarded the Burma Star. After being 'blown up', his brothers Dougie and Ronnie had lived to tell the tale. Emmie thought they were all heroes.

One day, Emmie took out the photo of her Girls Life Brigade cadets, taken on the occasion when she took them to spend a day at the boys' camp. She always thought of them as 'my' cadets.

"It's just as well none of us knew what they would have to face," thought Emmie. She was very proud of them. Her gaze lingered on them one by one. Edna Dickson had been so happy in her Land Army duties that she intended to stay on the farm. Some of the cadets were married. Joan Beatson had come home from the Signal Corps in the A.T.S. at Salisbury to be married at St. Swithin's soon after VE Day. Her husband, Alan Green, had been in the RAF, training in Canada and then transferred to the Far East. Emmie thought how widely people had travelled and wondered if

it would be difficult for them to settle down. Marie Hault smiled out of the photograph and Emmie immediately thought of Maisie Wolfenden. The two little girls had been so close that it was hard to think of one without the other. They lived in adjoining houses and used to tap messages on the fireback with the poker. They had both joined the Wrens and both became wartime brides in the same week in February 1945. Marie had married a Royal Engineer and moved away. Maisie had married a local boy, Don Prior. Don had been in Air-Sea Rescue. Like many others, he preferred not to speak about his war experiences.

Emmie had heard about Maisie's wedding from her father. Maisie had discovered that those who served in the Wrens could borrow a wedding dress from a film company. She had sent her measurements and received a fabulous dress. The company was not allowed to disclose the name of the star that had worn it. Maisie had looked wonderful on her wedding day with her groom very smart in uniform. Emmie's thoughts wandered to wartime weddings. Her old friend, Mary Battams, had had quite a glamorous wedding. Mary had grown from an adventurous tomboy into an elegant, long-legged blonde. She had become a model for C&A Modes, a very fashionable Sheffield store. Her wedding dress and all her bridesmaids' dresses were of her own design and made for her in the store. Mary had modelled numerous wedding dresses during her career. At last she was a real bride! Emmie hoped that Mary and all her old friends could be truly happy now that the war was over.

*   *   *   *   *

One Saturday morning in March, a familiar knock came at the door. Mr Wolfenden was delivering fruit and vegetables. He grinned at Emmie.

"There's a surprise for you," he said. "Where are the children?"

Emmie called them to the door and, like a conjuror, Mr Wolfenden pulled out three bananas! He gave them one each. They stared. Christine, always willing to try anything, opened her mouth to bite it.

"No!" squeaked Emmie, as Christine pulled a face. "You have to peel it first."

Eric was not sure if he remembered bananas. Enid didn't. All the children wanted Mum to have a bite of their banana. Mr Wolfenden chuckled. He was having a fine time with his consignment of bananas. Emmie and the children went to wave him off and to take Polly a crust. Polly was a gentle, dark brown horse, loved by all the customers. She always brought her forelegs on to the pavement in her eagerness for the expected offerings. She lowered her head for the children to stroke her nose. Mr Wolfenden climbed on to his cart and they waved goodbye.

"How kind of Mr Wolfenden to save you all a banana," said Emmie.

Life was gradually returning to normal. Billy dismantled the air-raid shelter. He positioned the four arch-shaped pieces of corrugated iron against the steep bank in the garden, one above the other. It formed a wavy slide for the children. It was just like a funfair! Emmie's garden was always full of children and the news of the slide in the Richardsons' garden spread quickly. The three Kenny boys came through the hedge at the bottom of the garden. June Paulie, and Jean and Carol Dickinson came from across the road. Children kept arriving. Emmie found old doormats and battered tin trays for them to slide on. She gave out old newspapers. When Enid's friend Tony came, Emmie said regretfully, "I'm sorry Tony. I haven't anything left for you to slide on. Run home and ask your mother to find you something."

It was a wonderful day and the sun blazed down. The metal slide became hotter and slippier. Shouts of laughter and excitement echoed around Essex Road.

The children whooped with delight as they slid to the bottom and tirelessly climbed the garden path. Round and round they went, hardly stopping for lunch and tea. At bedtime, parents came to coax their children away. Eric, Enid and Christine came in looking healthy after a long day in the fresh air. Their cheeks were rosy and as they sat in their pyjamas drinking cocoa, Emmie thought how contented they all were. At this moment, there was a knock at the door and Tony's mother appeared dragging a very reluctant Tony. To his embarrassment, he was turned round and bent over to display the large holes in his trousers, and a scarlet bottom. His mother pulled his trousers down to his ankles and said crossly, "Look at our Tony!"

The children looked. Tony tried to object to being doubled up with his bottom exposed but his mother gripped him more tightly and continued her tirade. Emmie tried to apologise and explain. She had always had happy relationships with her neighbours. The children found it hard to restrain their mirth at poor Tony's discomfiture and buried their noses in their cocoa cups. Eventually Tony's mother, somewhat mollified, hustled Tony outside. They could hear her sharp voice accusing him of not doing 'as you were told!' Tony was in for an uncomfortable night.

Billy took the slide down in spite of his children's' protests.

"I did tell you it couldn't stay here for ever," he reminded them. Ah well! What a glorious day it had been. They would always remember the slide, and certainly the sight of poor old Tony's bottom would amuse them for years.

There was always something to laugh about. Hearing a knock at the door one day, Enid and Christine ran to open it. Their father, hoping to amuse his ballet-stricken daughters, stood there in a perfect 'fifth position', his arms held daintily over his head and a smirk on his face. This pose was made more impressive by the coal-blackened face, the grease-covered boiler suit and the heavy pit boots. The girls shrieked with laughter and Emmie came to admire him.

"Do a plié, Daddy," said Christine. Billy obligingly bent his knees and then executed a few elegant polka steps. The children adored him.

It was good to have a proper family life again. Billy still worked long hours and studied too at regular night classes, but the exhaustion and anxiety of Home Guard duty and fire-watching was in the past. Life fell into a routine, which gave a sense of security. On Sundays the children attended Sunday school at Deep Pits and took part in many of the activities Emmie and Billy had known as children. It was their turn now to sit on the Anniversary platform and to follow the banner at

Whitsuntide. Then came a new addition to the family. Emmie rescued a little black pup found running between the traffic on Granville Road. He seemed to be a cross between a spaniel and a collie with long, silky ears and a white chest. The children ignored any mongrel qualities and gave him the grand name of Prince.

In the summer Billy decided that, although he could not take a week away from work, his family deserved a holiday. He planned to tow the caravan to Skegness. He warned the children that this would not be easy. The problem was that new tyres were unavailable and the tyres on the Morris Eight were decidedly dilapidated. The inner tubes were old and patched. Eric watched his father cut strips to make 'gaiters' from unuseable, worn-out tyres and insert them into the old tyres. Five old inner tubes were packed with the tools and at last they were ready. It was a squash in the little car. Eric sat with Grandma in the front seat. Emmie squeezed between Enid and Christine in the back. They took turns to nurse the dog. It was exciting to tow for the first time. Enid and Christine sang, over and over again,

The little Morris Eight
Is pulling all the weight.

They set off in a spirit of adventure, which was a good thing because the journey was not easy. Eight times Billy pulled in and mended punctures. The gaiters helped to pad out the tyres but they moved against the inner tubes, making holes worse.

Finally Billy drove on to a grass verge and said, "Everybody out!"

The children were glad to tumble out. It was their turn to help. "You must all gather grass, "Billy told them, "and bring it to me." The tyres were removed again and each one was stuffed with grass. "Well done!" praised Billy. "Everyone back in again."

The last leg of the journey was made with one tyre completely flat, but at last the caravan was towed onto the site. Everybody cheered!

Emily, Emmie and the children enjoyed a week at the seaside, and Billy came to spend a couple of days with them before the return journey. On Friday morning, leaving Grandma to rest, they walked to the sea front. The weather was not perfect but many families strolled along breathing in the sea air. It was good just to be alive!

187

"Oh, I do like to be beside the seaside!" sang Emmie. As they walked along hand in hand, a seaside photographer snapped them and gave Emmie a ticket. "Thank you," she said. "We'll collect it from the kiosk later." The tiny snapshot, printed '*Skegness 1946*', was one to treasure. The horrors of war behind them, the family smiled into the camera, and into the future. The future looked bright.

Epilogue

S o did they live happily ever after? Yes, they did. They did not stay at Essex Road but kept close contact with Deep Pits. 1948 brought a move to Woodhouse where, once again, Emmie could see cows at the bottom of the garden. Her children could run down a steep path through a tunnel of trees to a bluebell wood with a stream running along the valley. There was room to keep bantams as well as a dog, a cat, and a rabbit. For many years, the children's adored Grandma Evans divided her time between their home and her own at Deep Pits. That way she could still be near her sisters and attend her beloved chapel. The children could still go to Grandma's for tea. But she loved to be with the family at Vicar Lane, making sure her grandchildren behaved properly, cooking for them and taking an interest in all that they did. Occasionally she showed them her superior skills. Eric, learning to shoot, was taking pot-shots at tin cans balanced on the wall. Taking the gun from him, she neatly shot a pear from the tree by its stem. Then she demonstrated how she could shoot out a candle flame. Not many children had a grandma who was a cross between Delia Smith and Annie-get-your-gun!

Billy continued to study and in the fifties he became a chartered mechanical engineer, by the mature candidate route, after submission of a detailed engineering thesis. At this time he was a member of the Association of Mining, Electrical and Mechanical Engineers, and the Institution of Mining Engineers. As a result his designatory title became: W. Richardson, C. Eng, MI MechE, MI MinE, FI MEME.

Billy was deeply interested in his work and, as an Operations Mechanical Engineer for South Yorkshire, was responsible for the smooth running of many pits in the area. When he retired, he received a certificate for 'long and meritorious service in recognition of forty-seven years loyal and efficient service to the industry and the country.'

Billy was proud that his son and grandson followed in his footsteps.

Emmie was proud of all her family and was thrilled when her daughters became teachers. While they were away at college, she and Billy fostered two girls, Sylvia and Shirleen, and gave a student a home. There was always 'open house' for those in need. Around this time, they helped to form Brigade companies at Woodhouse St. Paul's Methodist where the family attended church. Later they moved to Dinnington to the Old Rectory. They were made very welcome at Anston Wells Methodist Church. Once again, they were called upon to help with Brigade companies.

Billy, now seventy, began to wonder if he was still a safe driver. To reassure himself, he took the advanced driving test at the age of seventy-one and passed. Sadly, a few years later he developed Parkinson's disease. He kept his mental alertness and his sense of humour, maintaining that the best way to stop shaking was to wield a screwdriver or a hammer. Emmie lost him on their fifty-seventh wedding anniversary.

Those who knew Emmie and Billy could hardly imagine one without the other, but through her Christian faith, Emmie had a remarkable strength. She continued to love her work with Sunday school and Brigade. Emmie was a very patient person but Sue Baggalley, who succeeded Emmie on her retirement as Captain of Girls Brigade, recalled the one occasion when she saw Emmie angry. They had taken the girls to Sheffield to take part in a big parade. Among the girls were a few newcomers who were not in full uniform. They looked smart and tidy in dark skirts and white shirts. An official, giving a pre-parade inspection, announced that these girls could not take part. Emmie's head went up.

"What do you think Jesus wants to see – girls or uniforms marching down the street?" The girls marched.

Emmie lived long enough to know and love seven grandchildren, eleven great-grandchildren and one great-great-grandchild. They all loved her.

Two weeks before her ninety-fourth birthday, Emmie died in her own home. Enid had visited her the night before and had been greeted by the lovely smile that everyone knew. The little church at Anston Wells was packed for her funeral. As at her wedding, there was a guard of honour by the Girls Brigade. The Brigade hats, which Emmie and Billy had worn with such pride, lay on her coffin. The flag she had followed for so many years followed her on her last journey. Emmie had always finished Brigade meetings with a prayer and the 'magic squeeze'. The girls wanted this ritual to take place at her funeral. All around the tightly packed church the congregation joined hands and an officer squeezed the hand of the person next to her. The squeeze was passed along from person to person, passing God's love around the church. It took some time to proceed, and heads were turned this way and that, hoping the 'squeeze' had not been lost. Then suddenly the officer announced, "Message received and understood." There was a burst of applause and a cheer went round the church. Emmie would have been glad to hear laughter at her funeral.

This book set out to tell the stories my mother used to tell, of her childhood and the community in which she grew up. It grew into a love story. It was written for Emmie and Billy and for all those who shared their lives. Above all, it was written for our grandchildren – Rebecca, Conal, Alexander, Cormac, and Patrick. Hopefully, it will reach other descendants of Walter and Ellen Bell, who lived at the old farmhouse where the story began.

ACKNOWLEDGEMENTS

My grateful thanks go to the Royal National Lifeboat Institution for their kind permission to use a photograph and material from their archives. Thanks also to Geoff Hall for sharing his life-long farming expertise.

My brother, Eric Richardson, deserves a special mention for his patient response to my many questions and for his amazing, detailed memories.

Thanks to my encouraging sister, Christine Strong, and to my cousin Neil.

I include many other relatives: Kenneth Bell, Dorothy Watson, Peter Bell, Joy Loughrey (nee Goodwin), Christine Newton, Betty Drake, Doris Boardman, John Bell, Rod Bell, Jacqueline Reid (nee Bell), Barbara Kent, Trevor Holmes, Dennis Goodman and Margaret Hardie.

I also thank Mary Hoyland (nee Battams) for special contributions and other former residents of Deep Pits: Edna Dickson, Joyce Martin (nee Cooper), Maisie Prior (neeWolfenden), Joan Green (nee Beatson), Marie Drew (nee Hault), Dorothy Athorne (nee Garret), Tom Oxley, Ron Wolfenden, Joan Jeffcock, Margaret Flint, Betty Parkin (nee Lakin) and Christine Staniforth.